T0041683

FROM THE FILMS OF

Harry Potter™

TRAVELS THROUGH THE WIZARDING WORLD

AN OFFICIAL COLORING BOOK

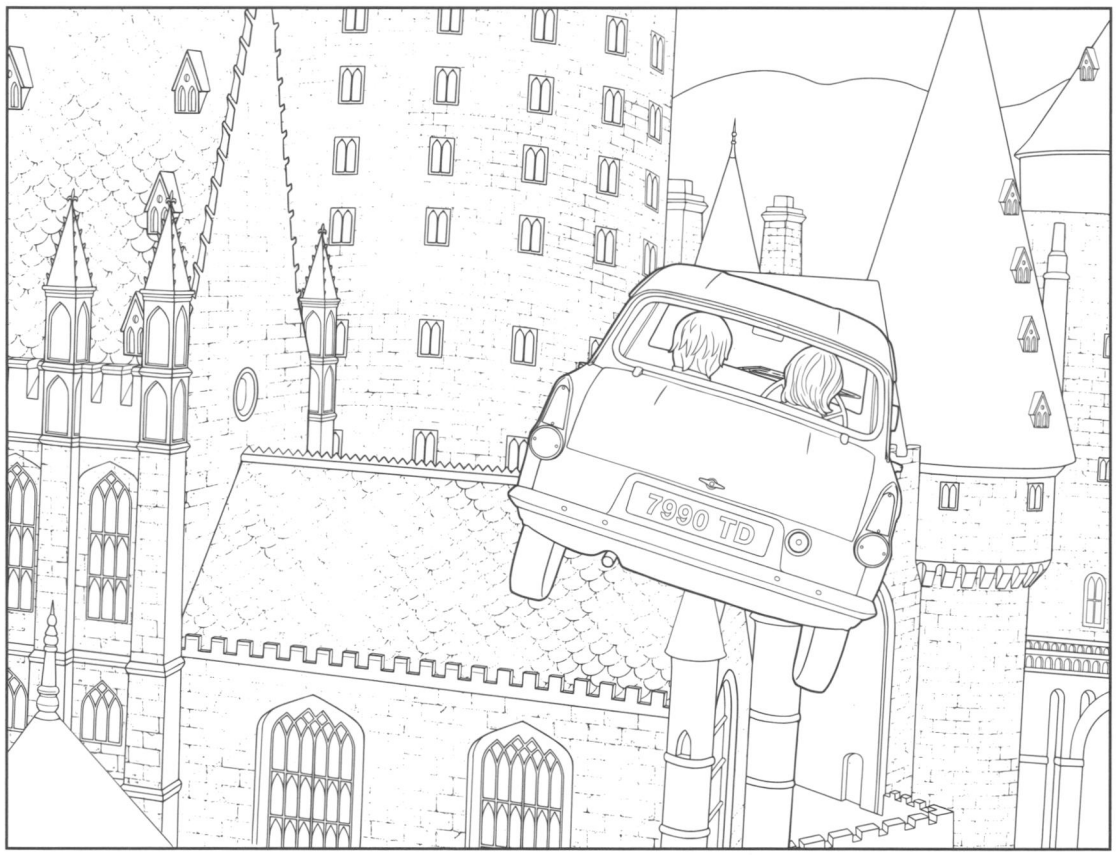

INSIGHT EDITIONS

San Rafael • Los Angeles • London

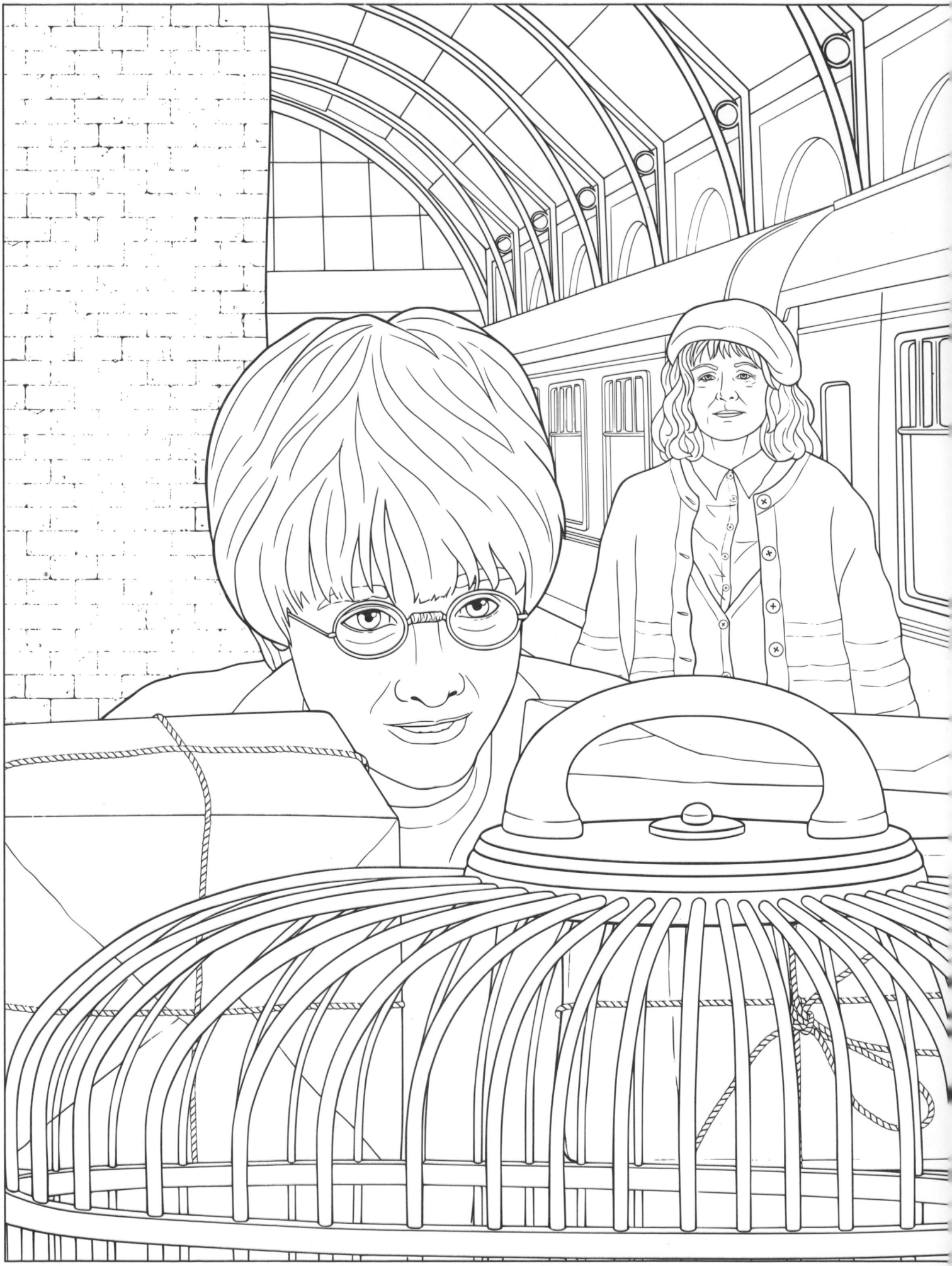

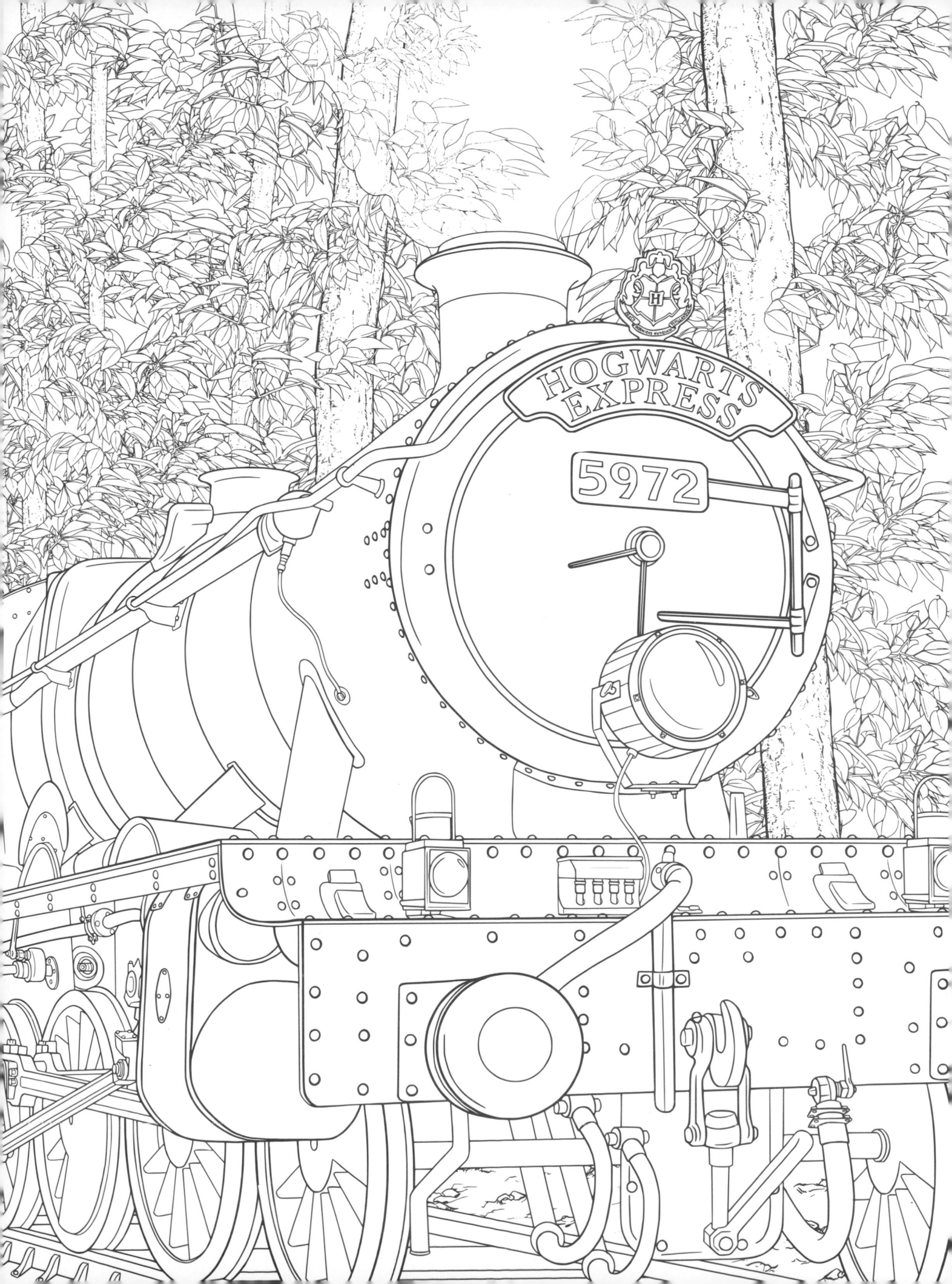
HOGWARTS
EXPRESS
5972

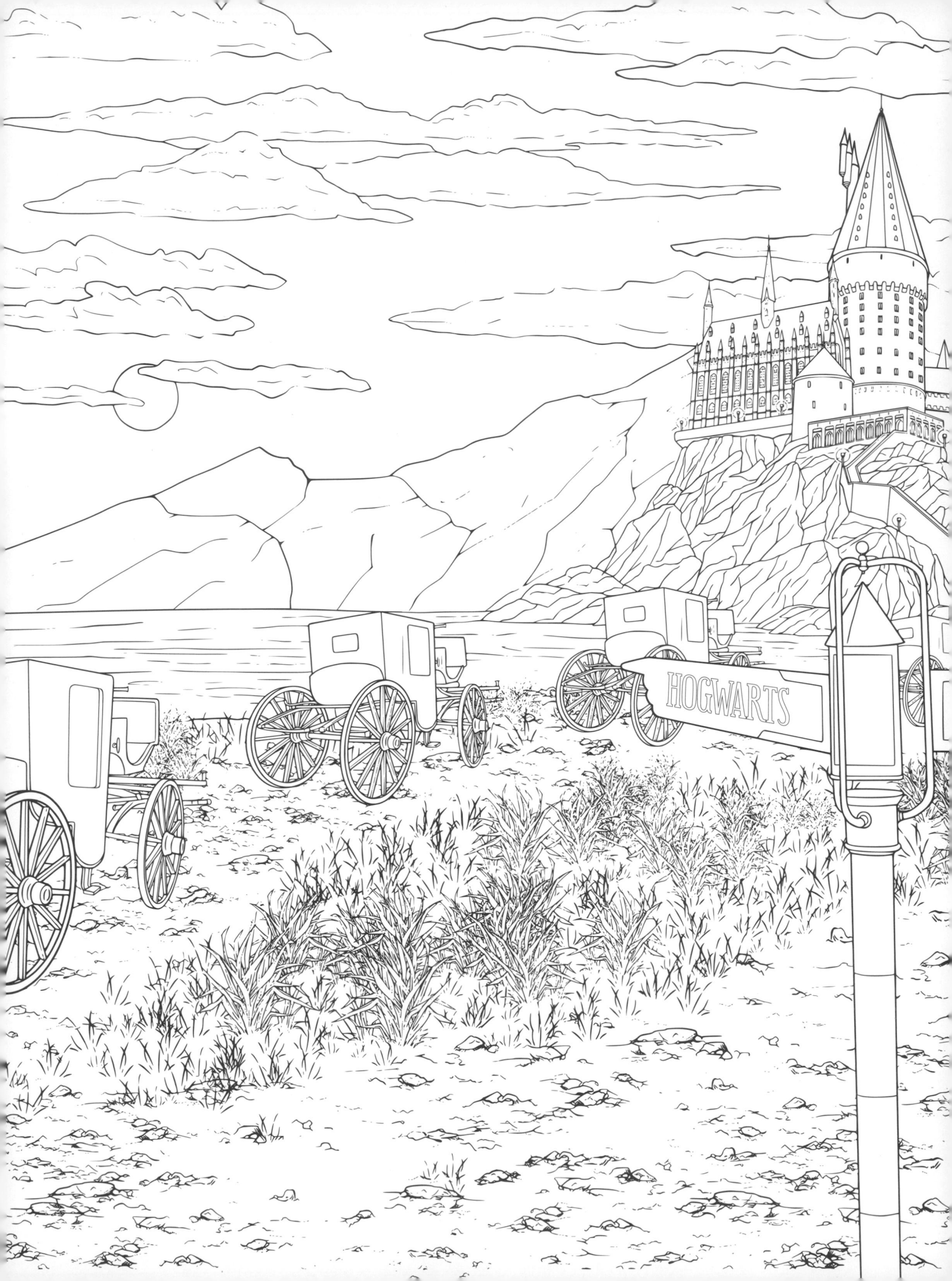
HOGWARTS

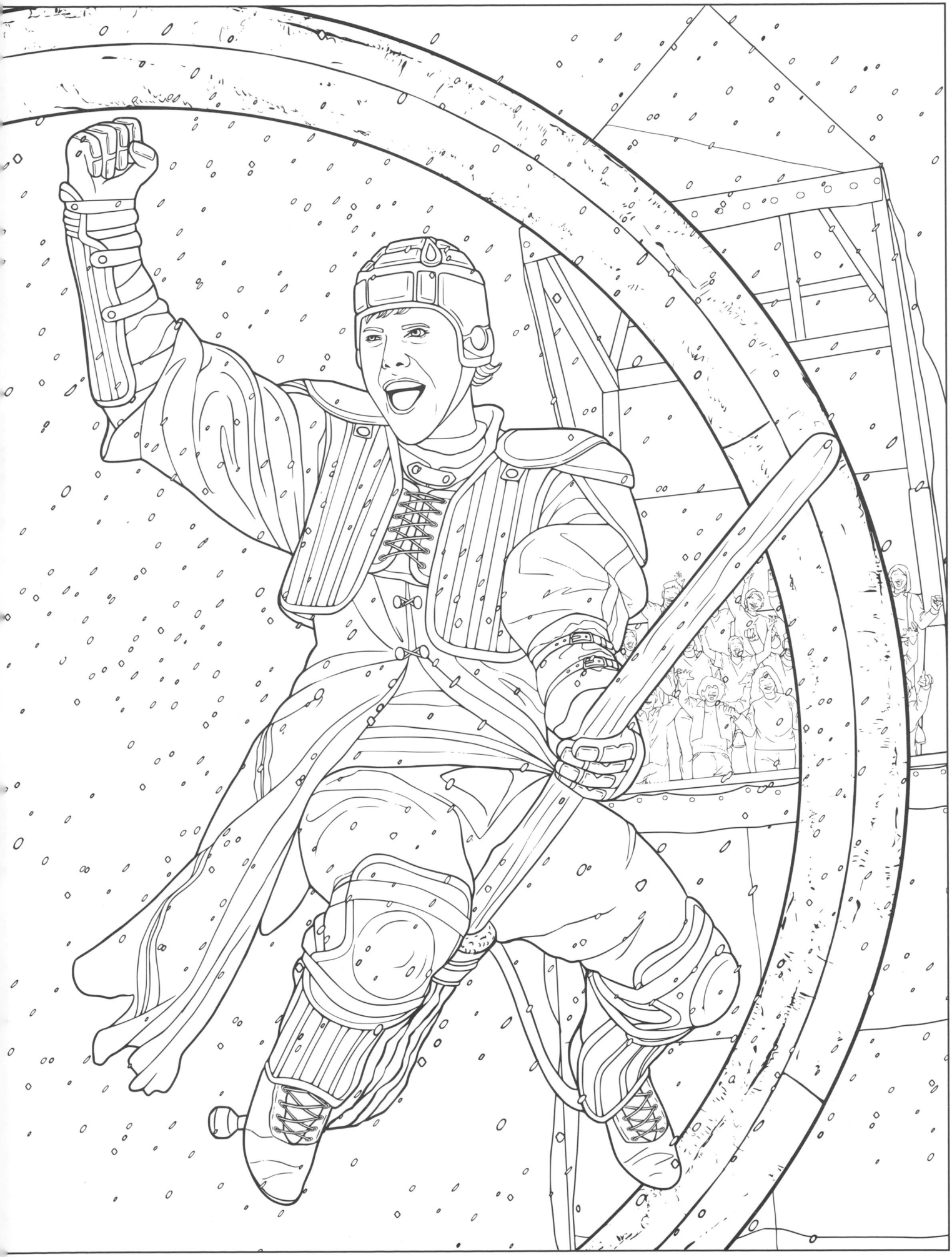

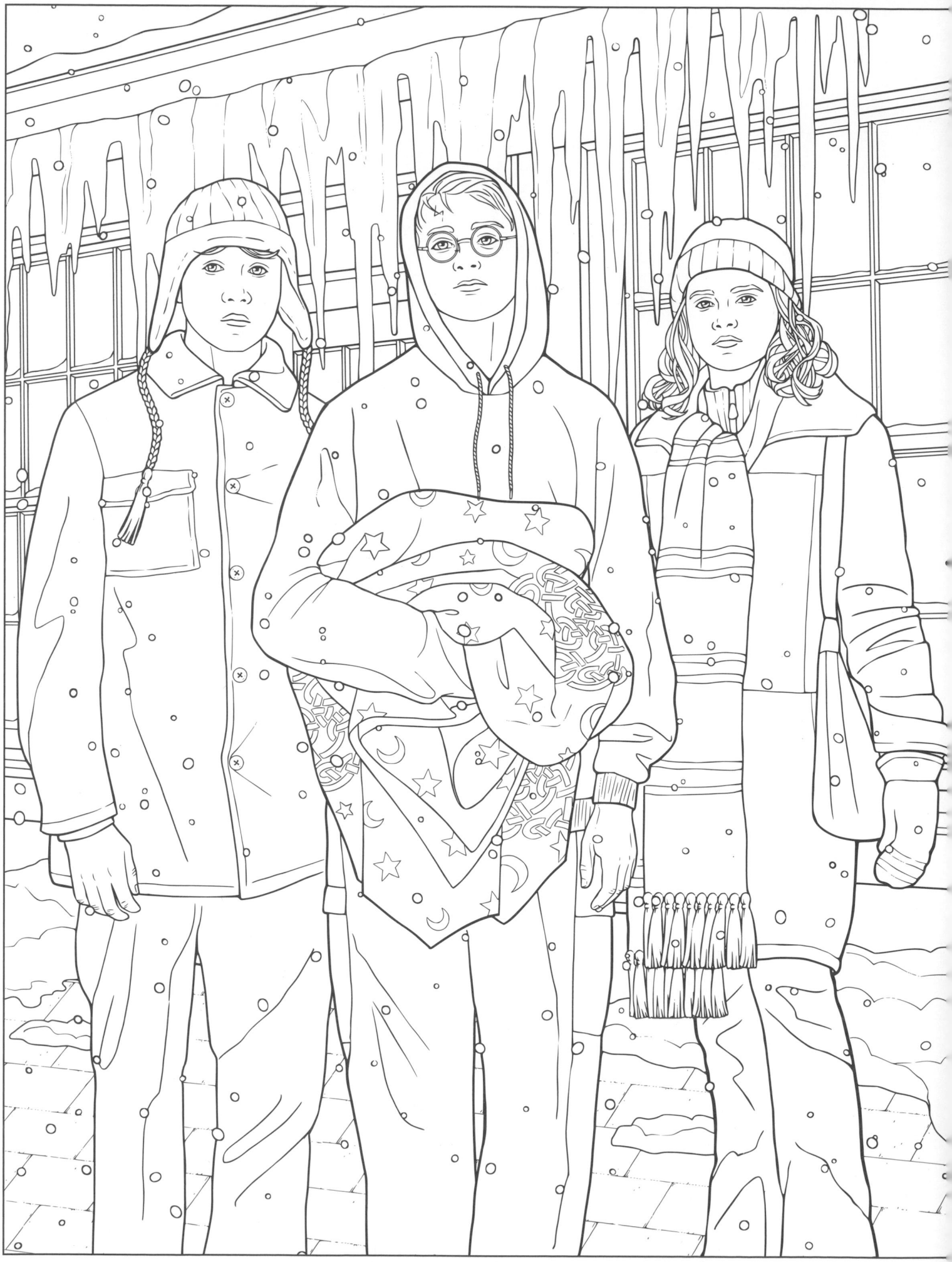

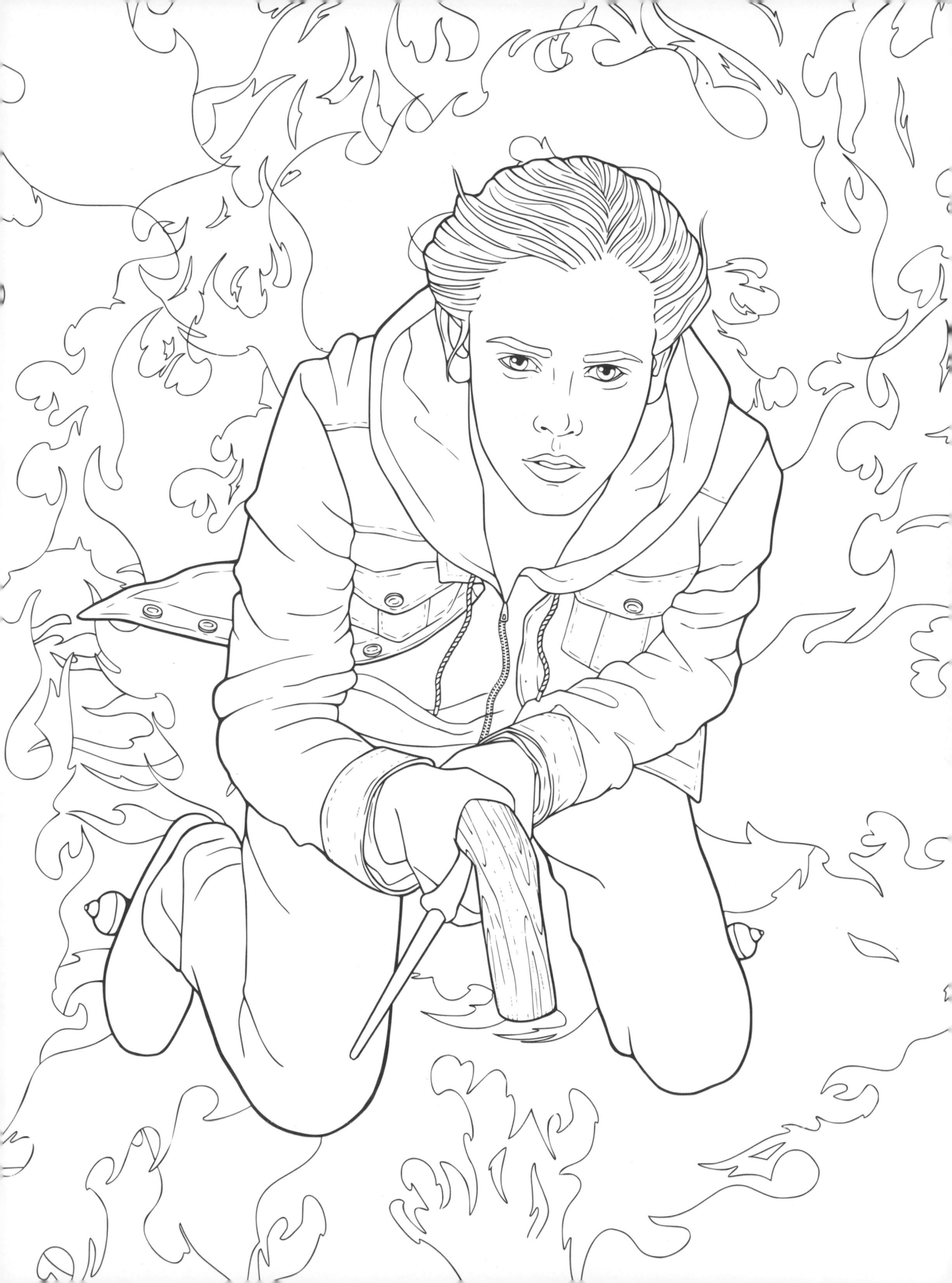

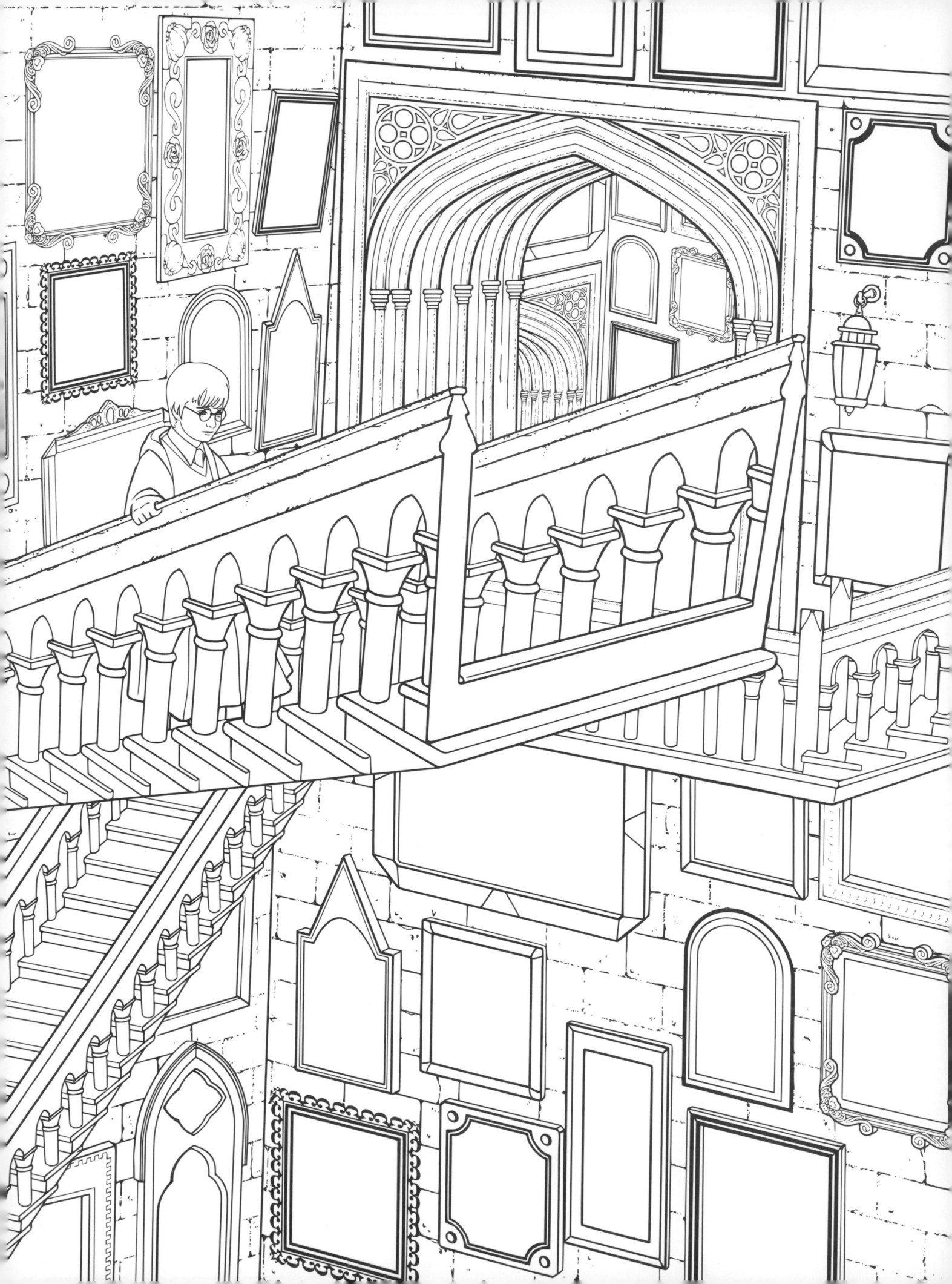

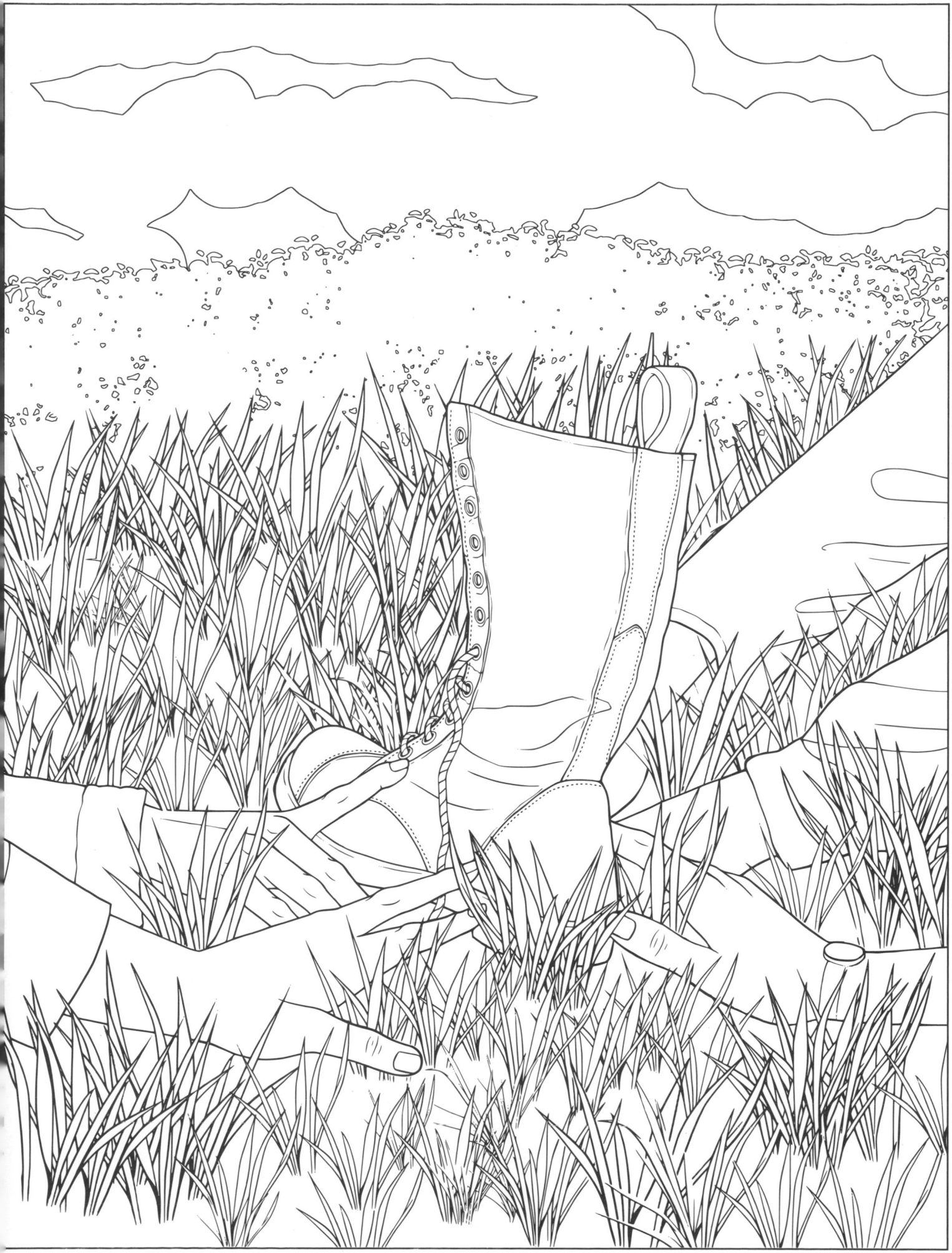

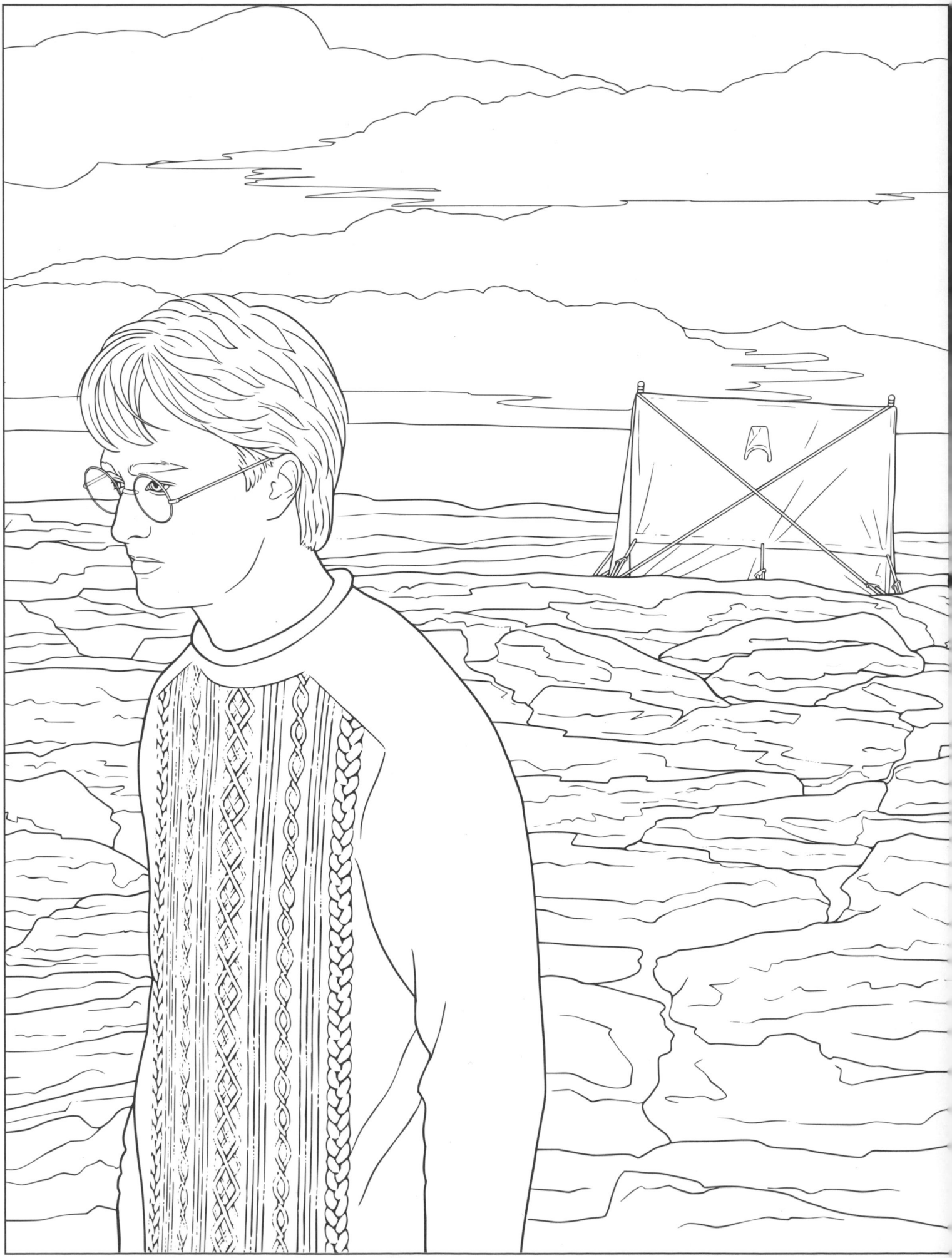

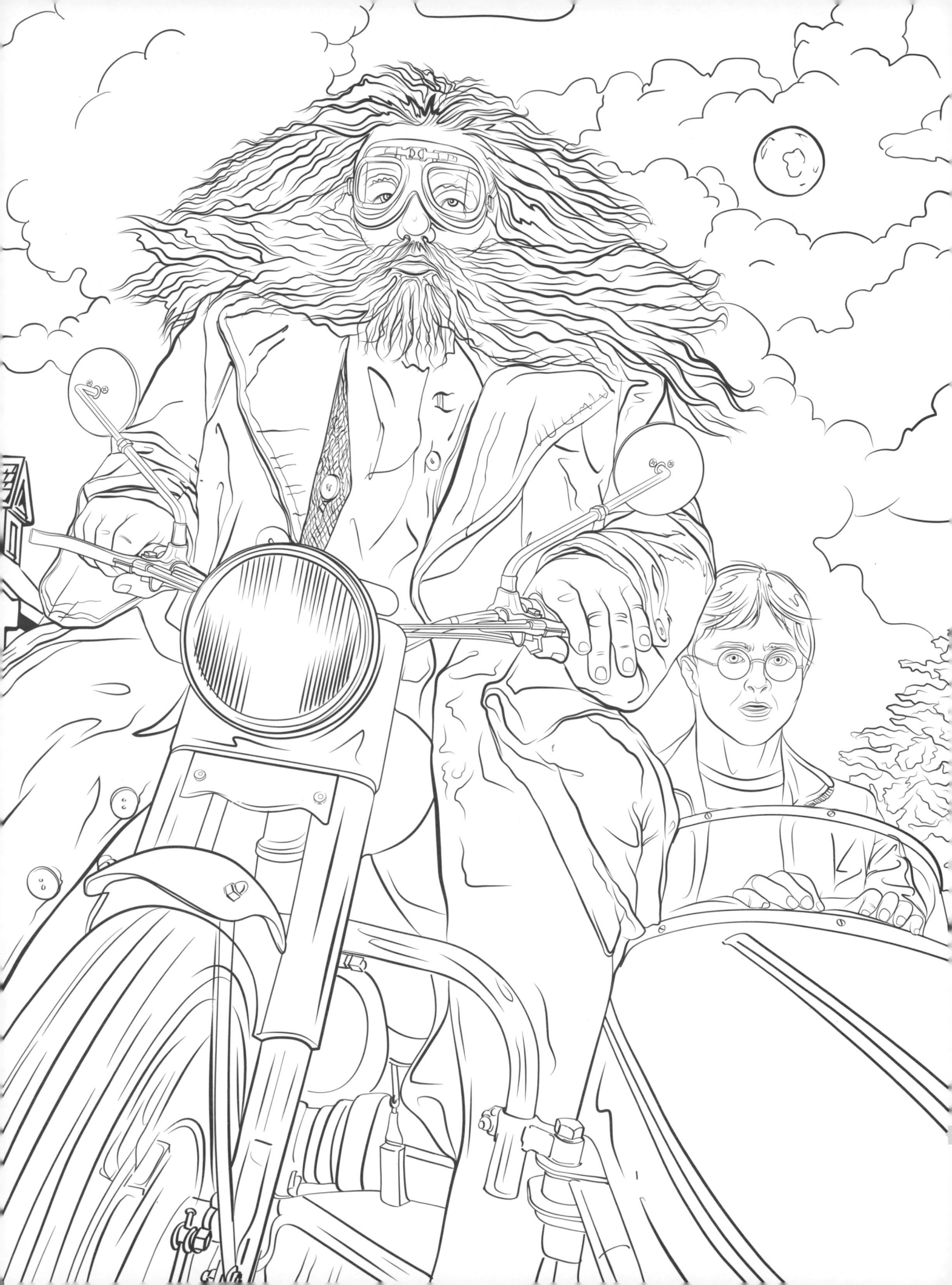

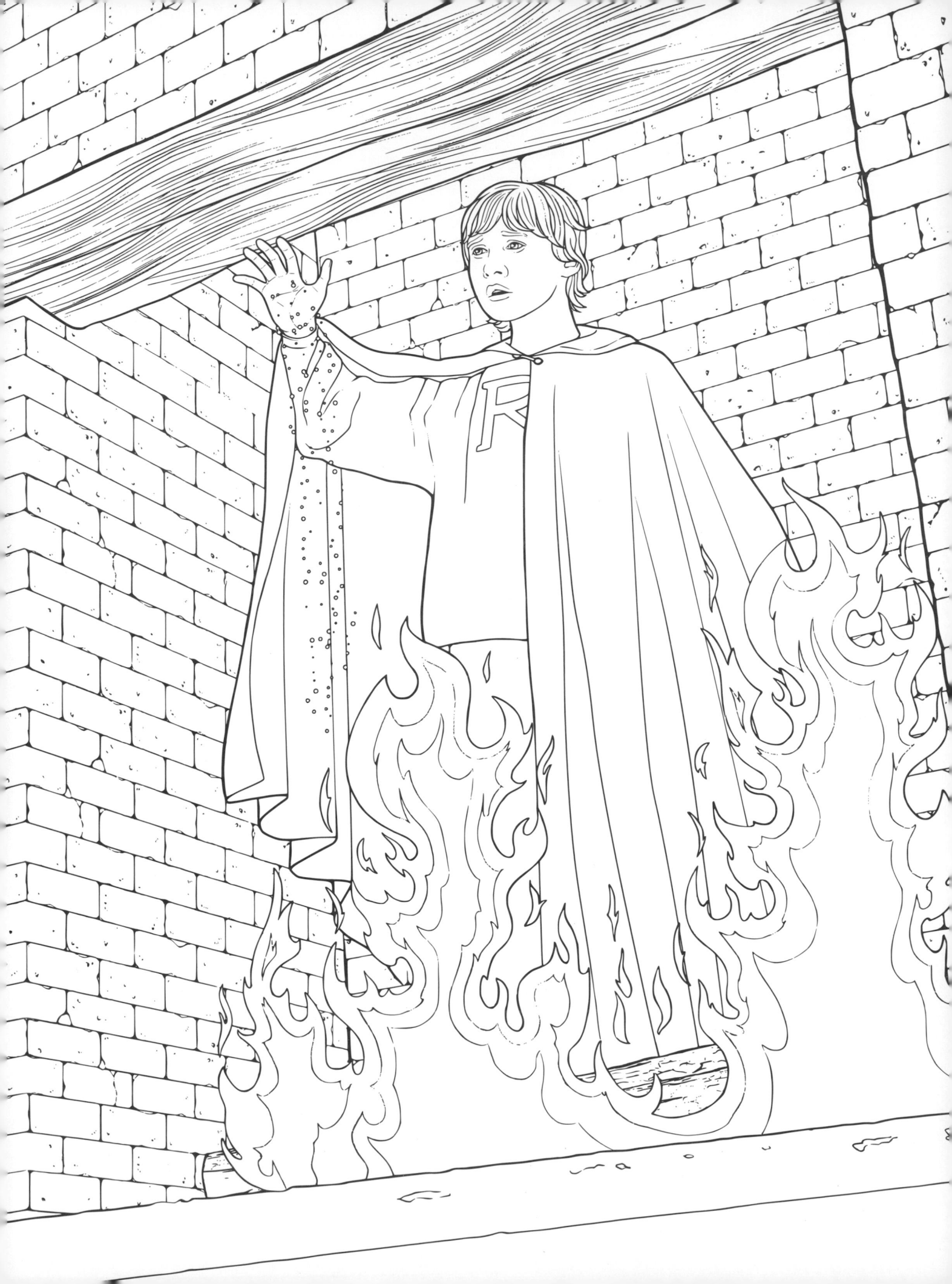

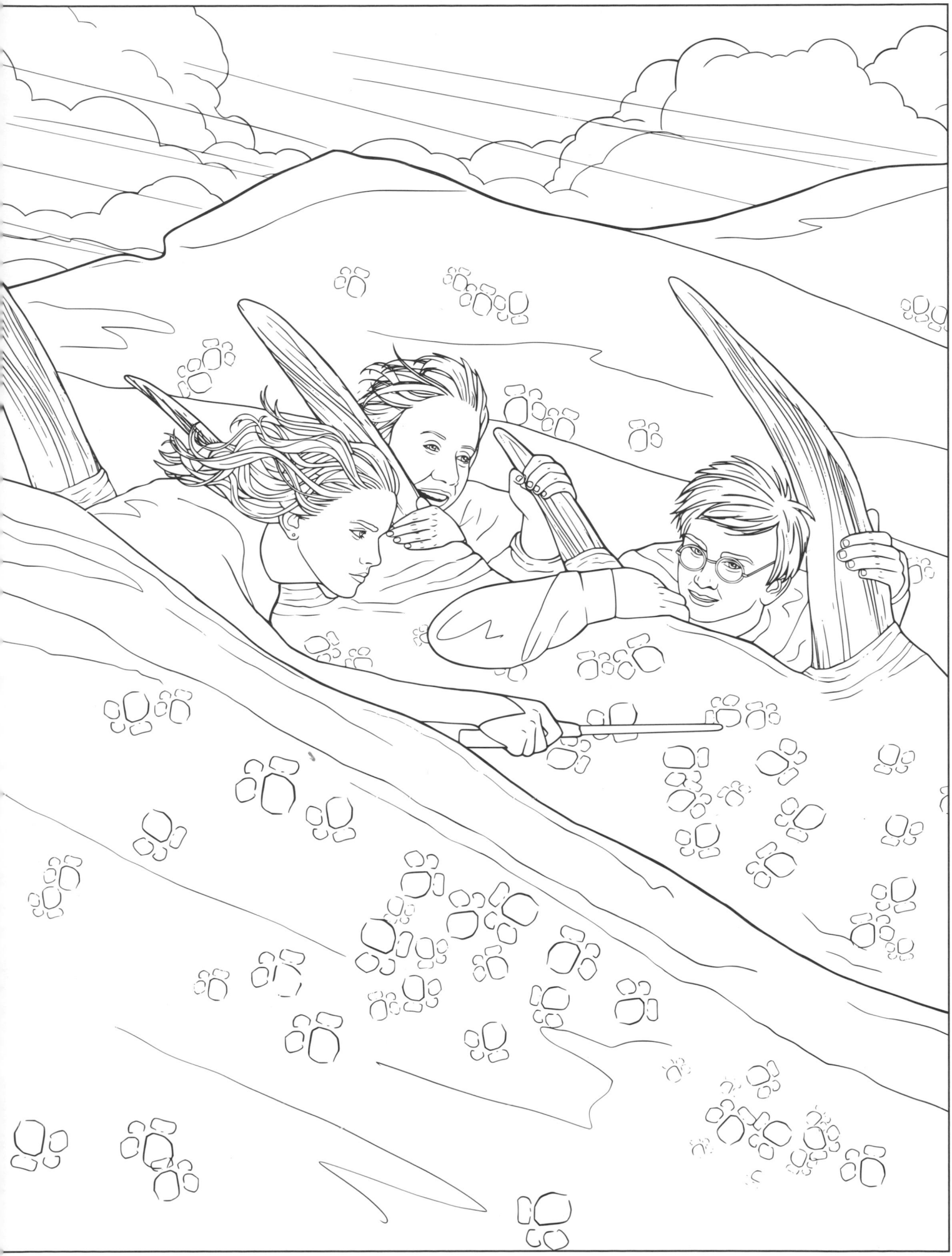

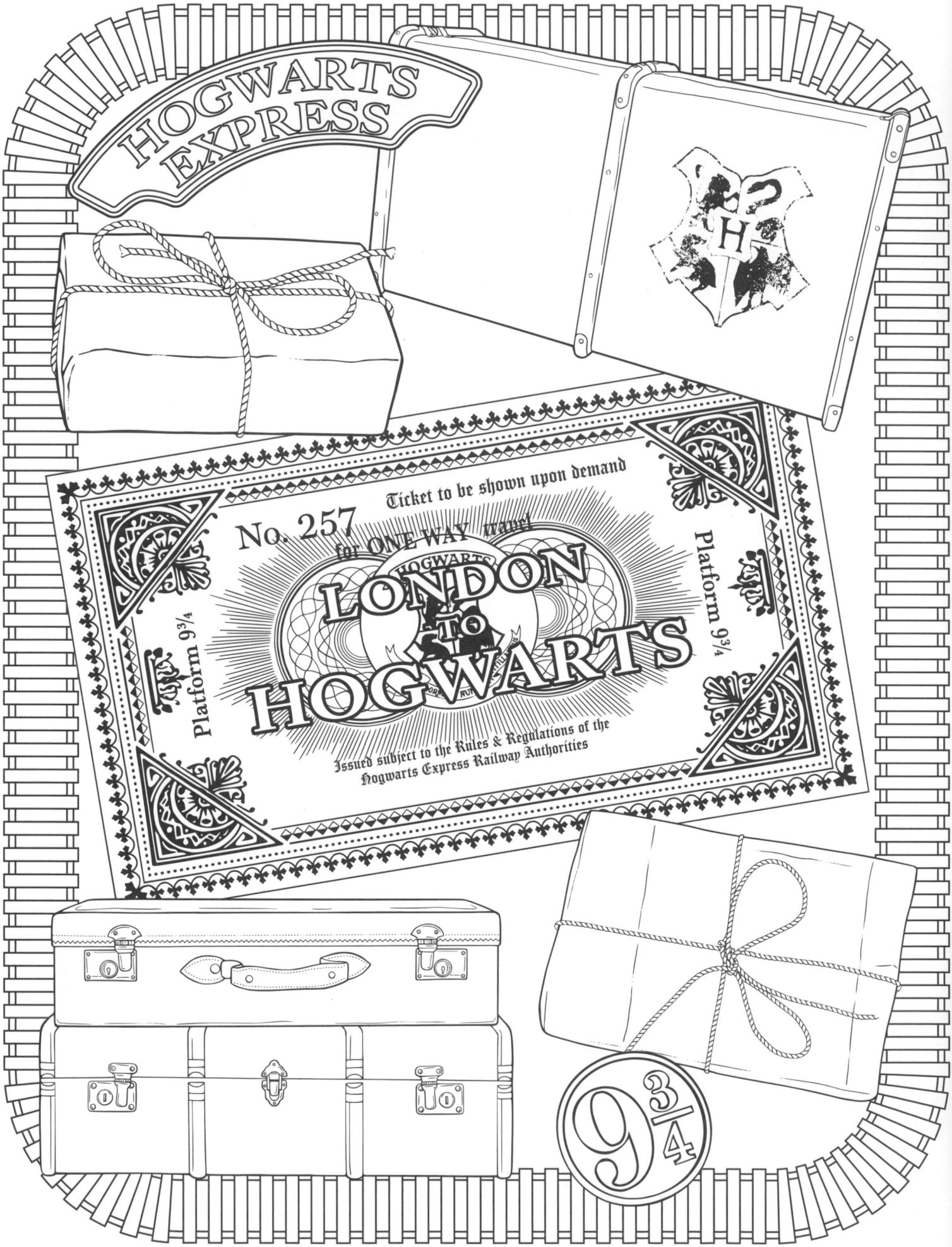
HOGWARTS EXPRESS
H
Ticket to be shown upon demand
No. 257
for ONE WAY travel
HOGWARTS
LONDON
TO
HOGWARTS
Platform 9¾
Platform 9¾
Issued subject to the Rules & Regulations of the
Hogwarts Express Railway Authorities
9¾

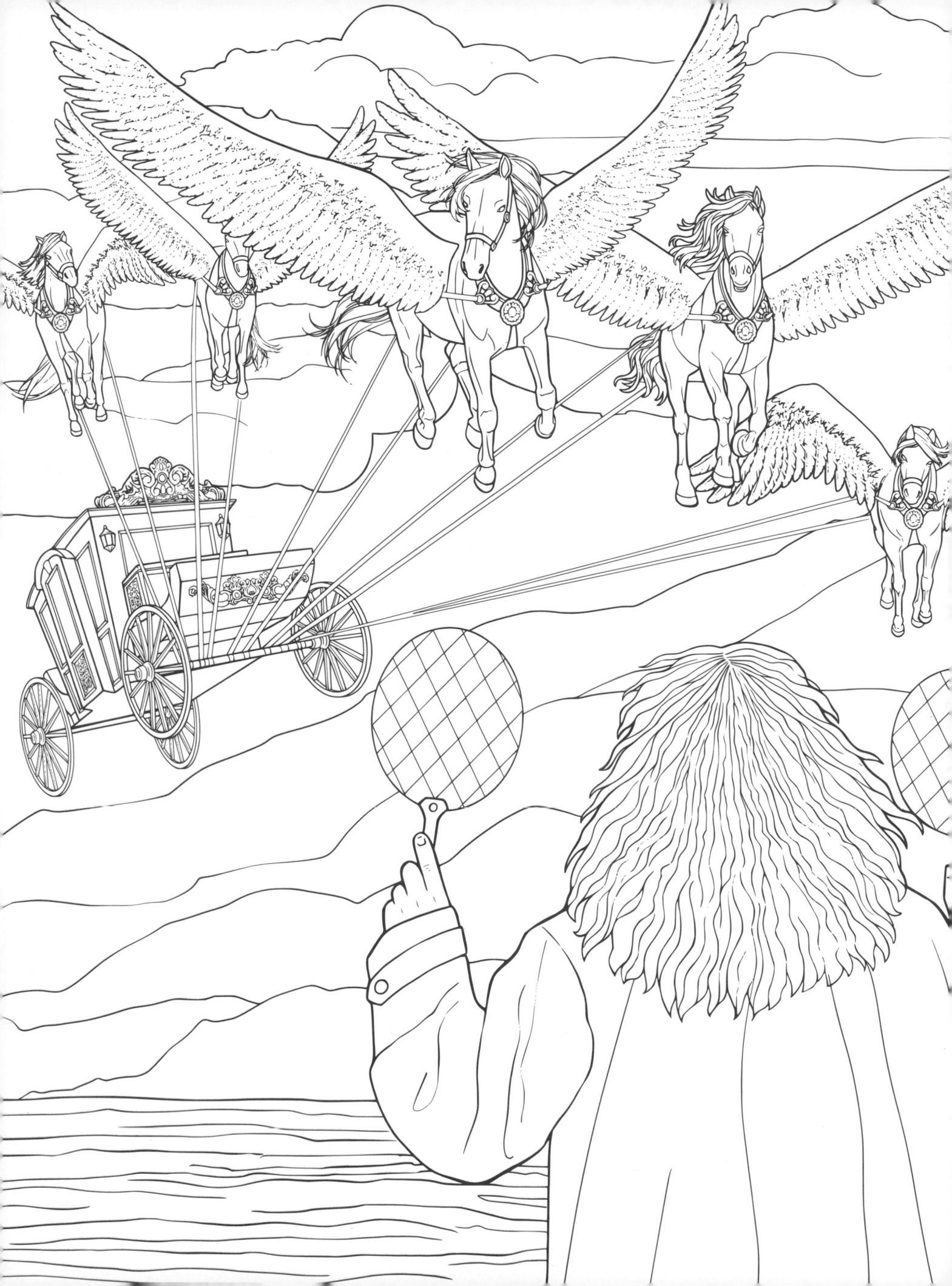

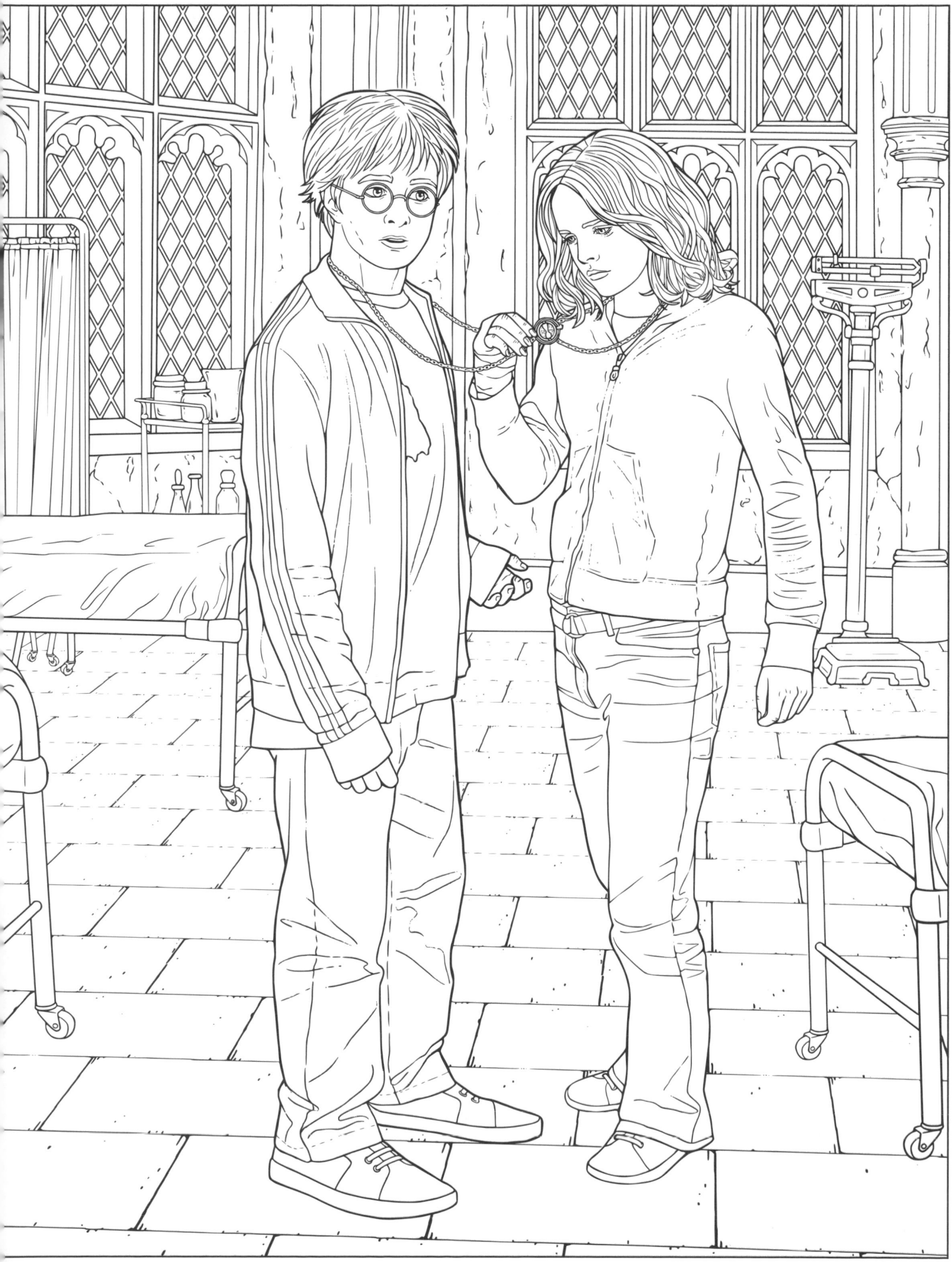

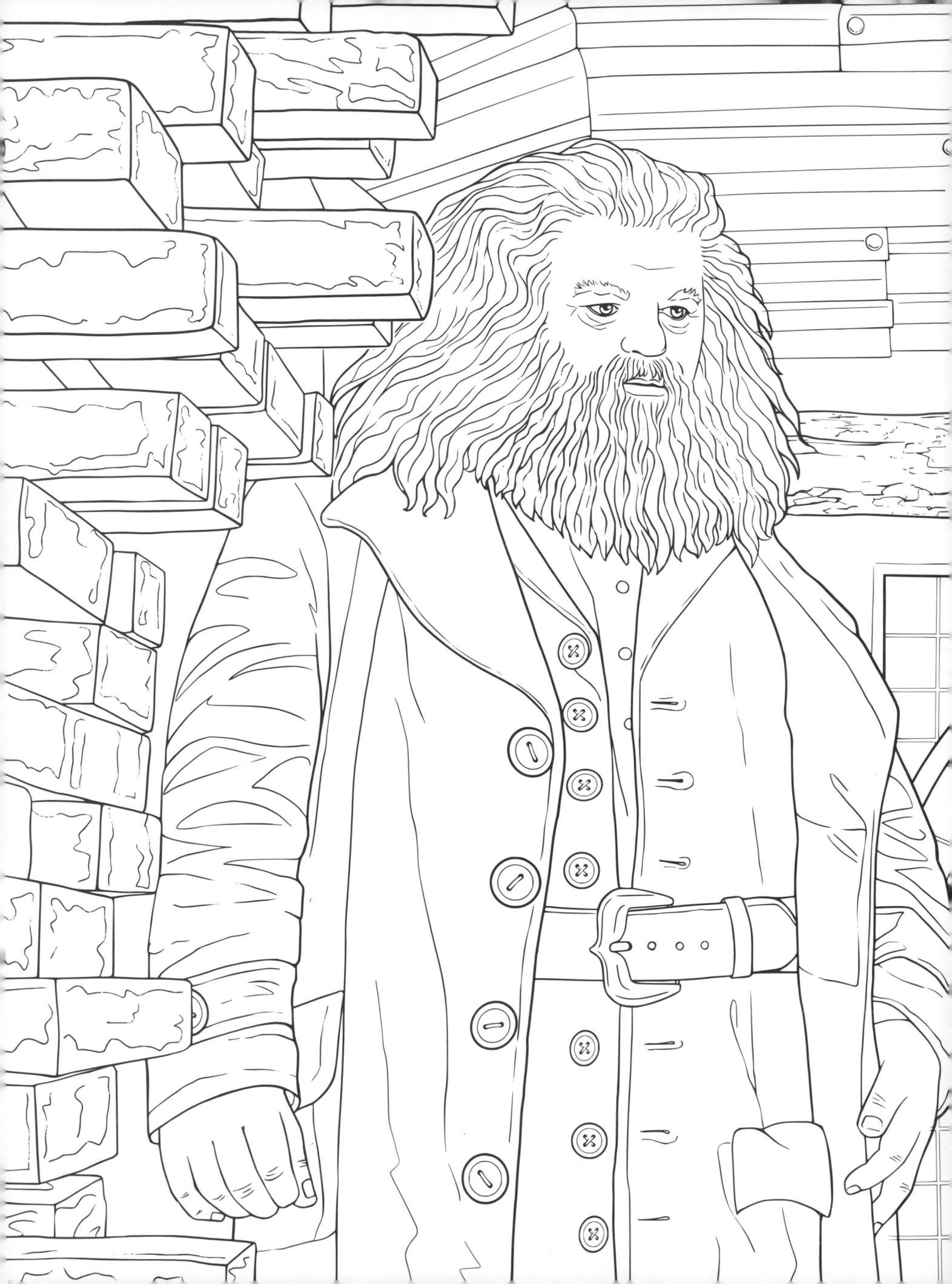

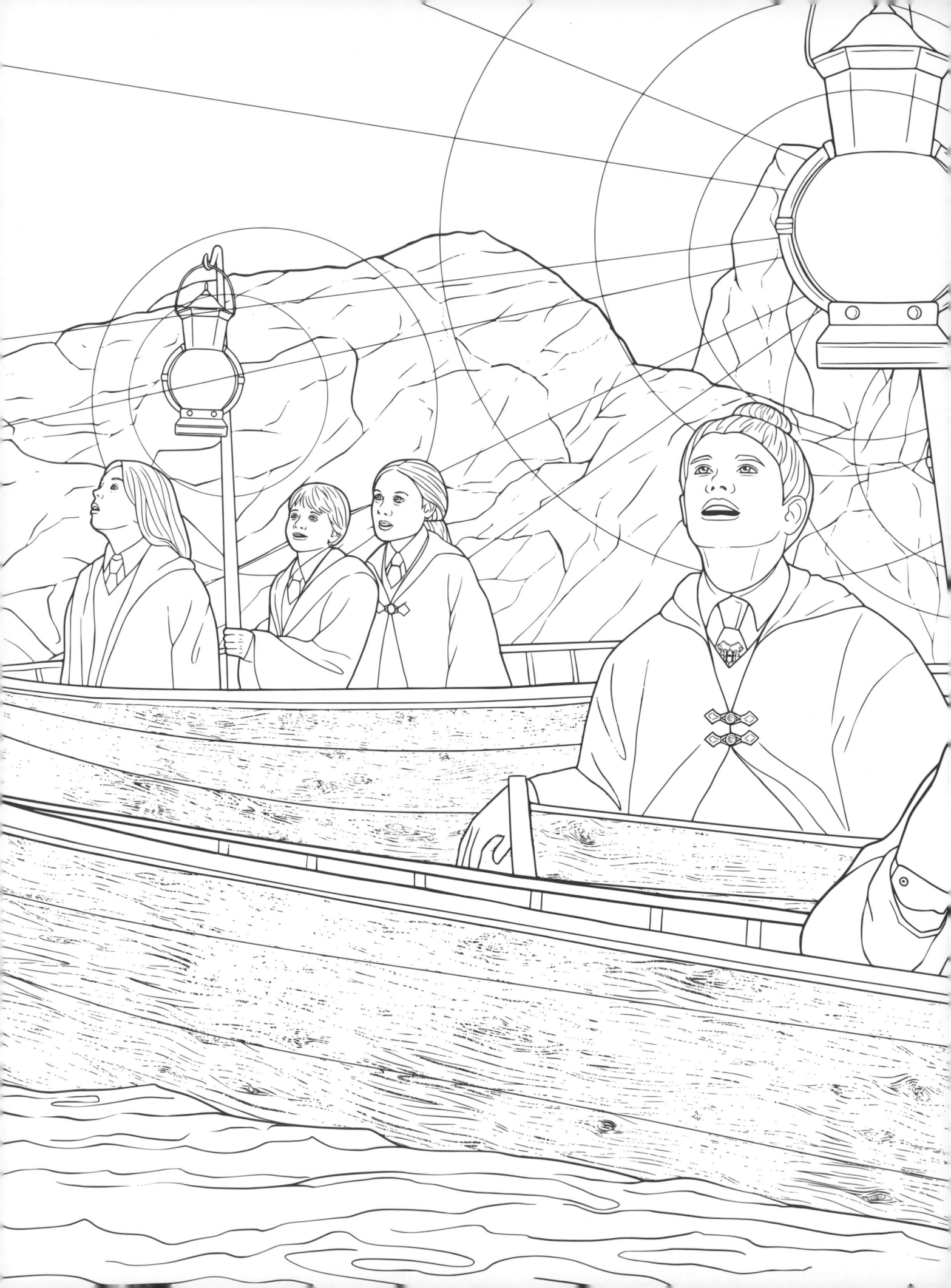

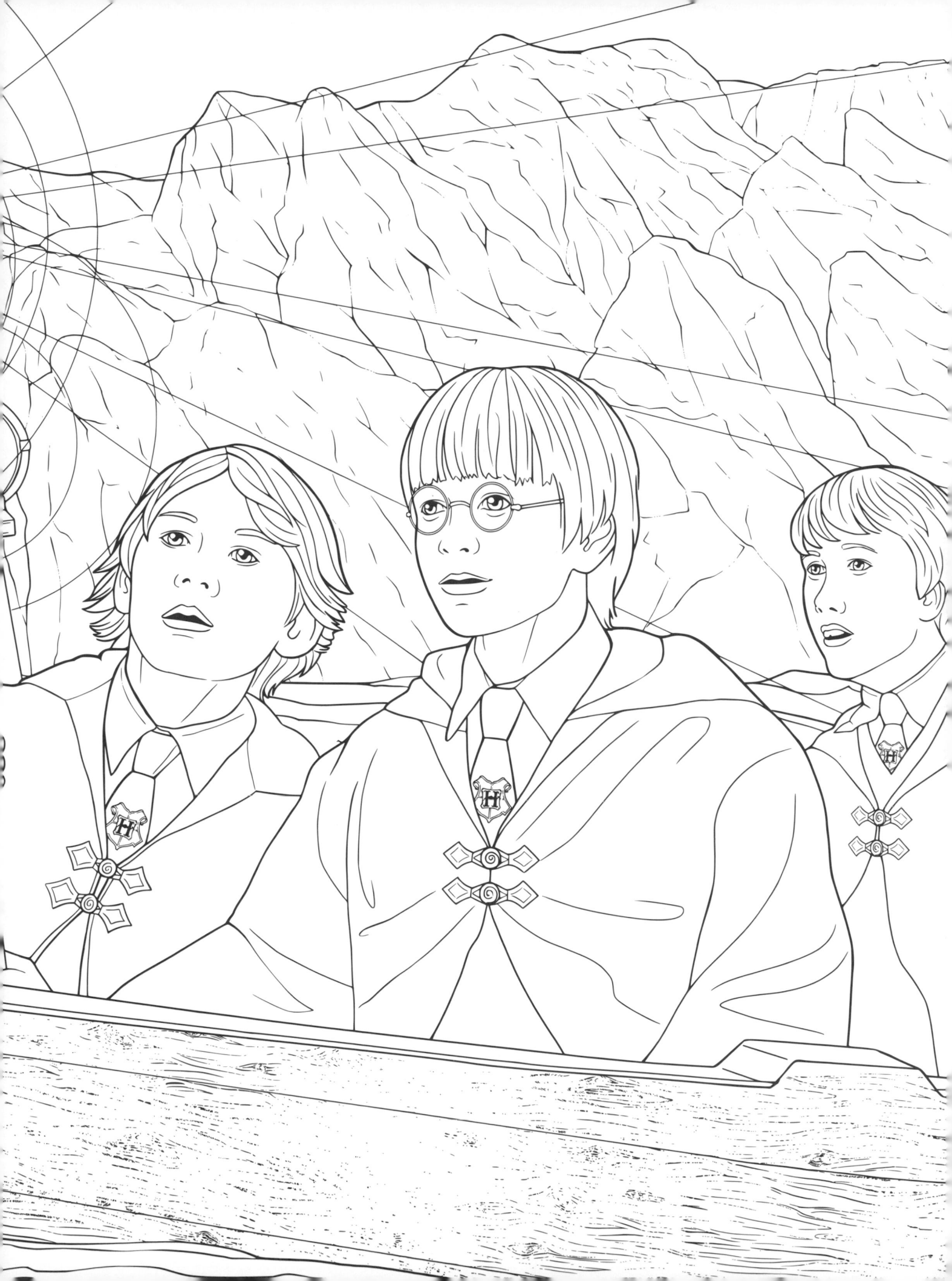

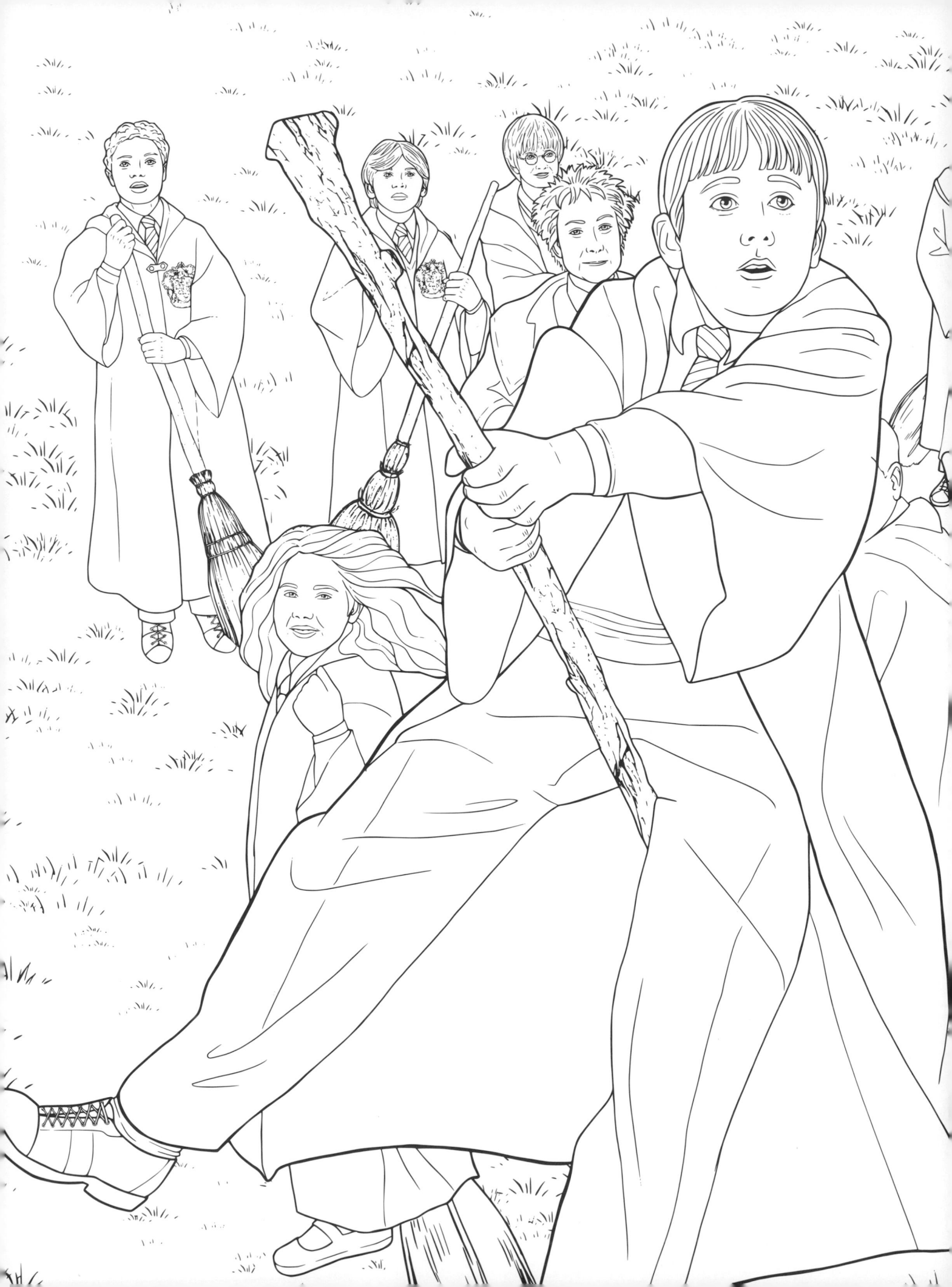

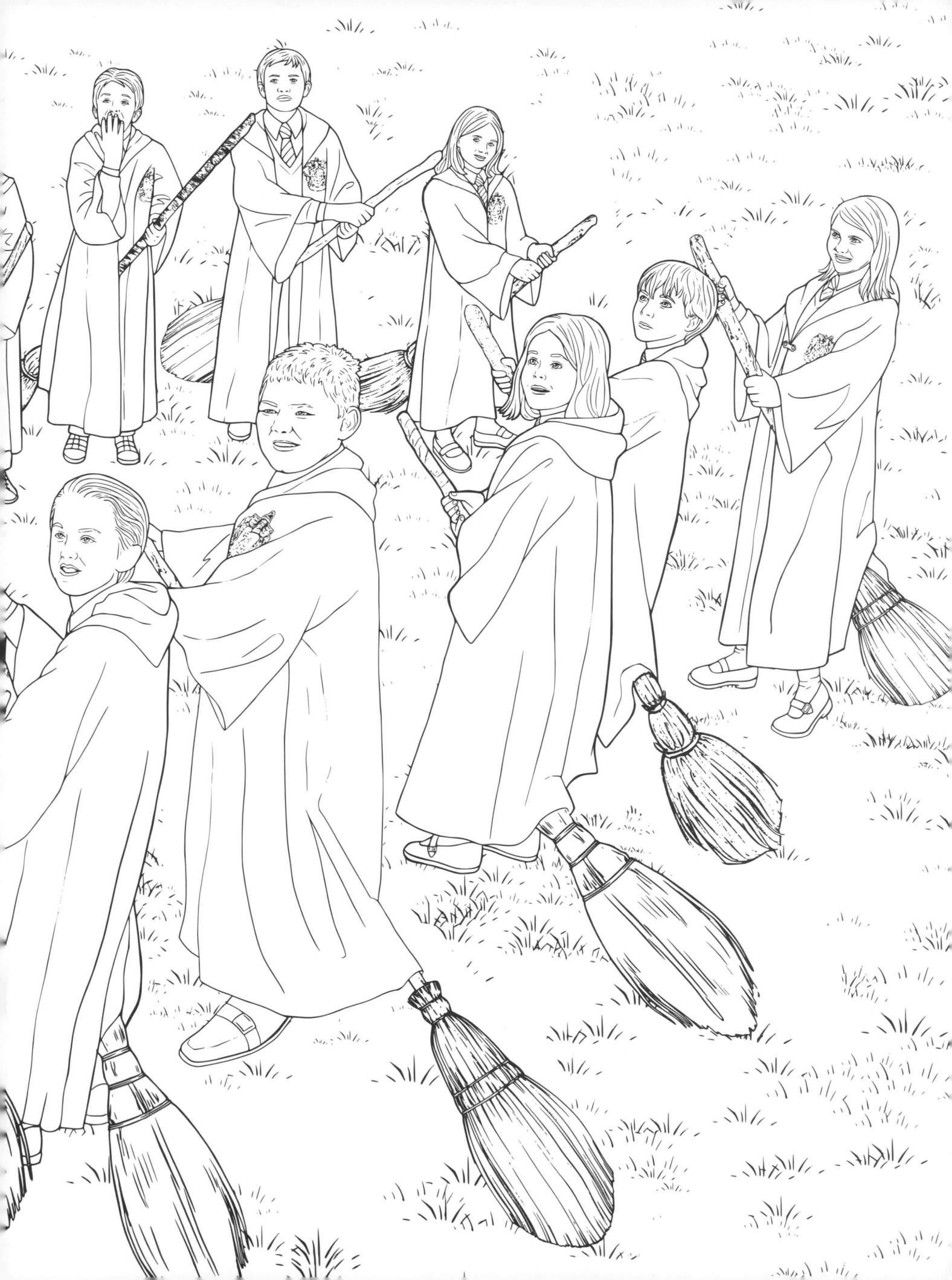

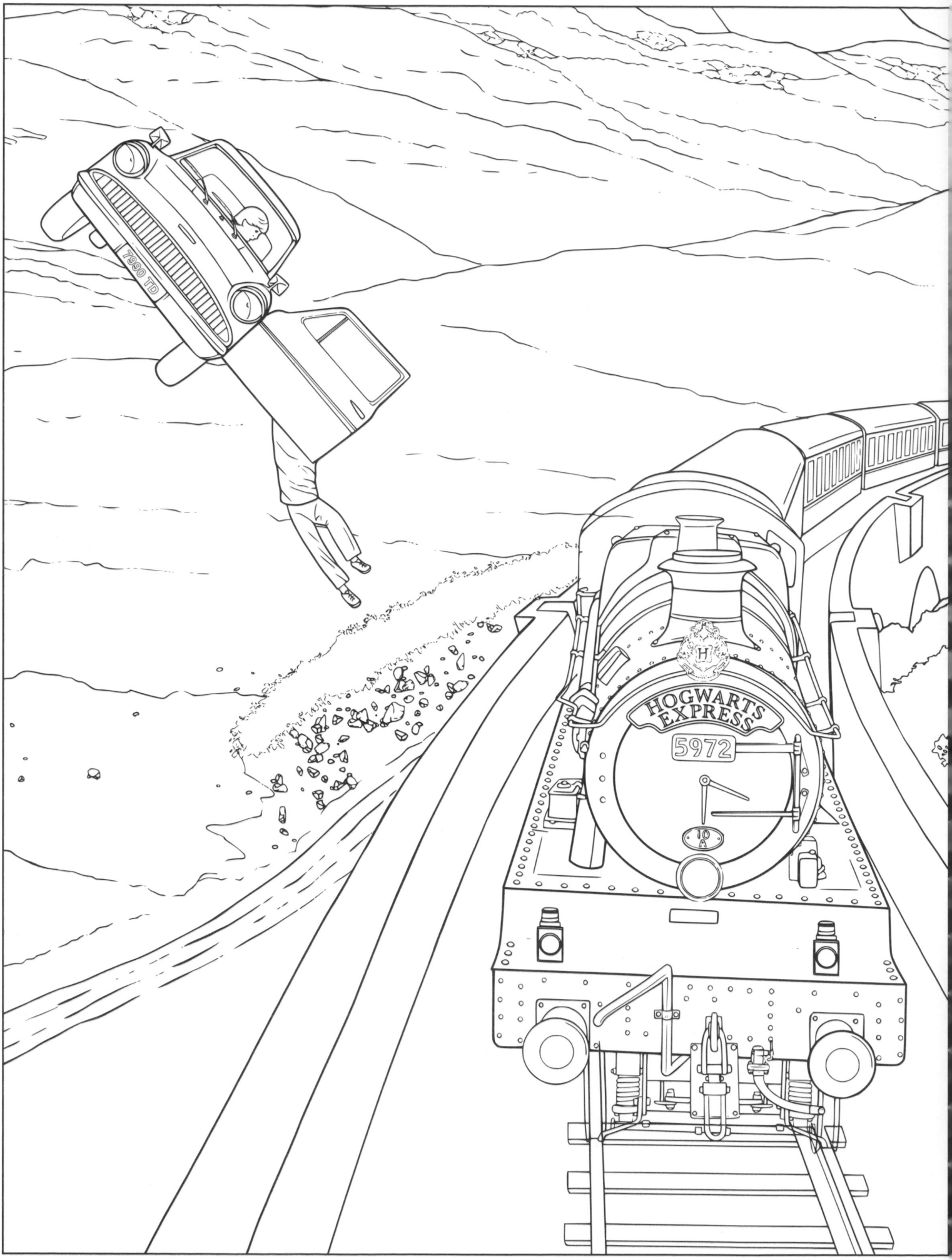
7990 TD
HOGWARTS EXPRESS
5972

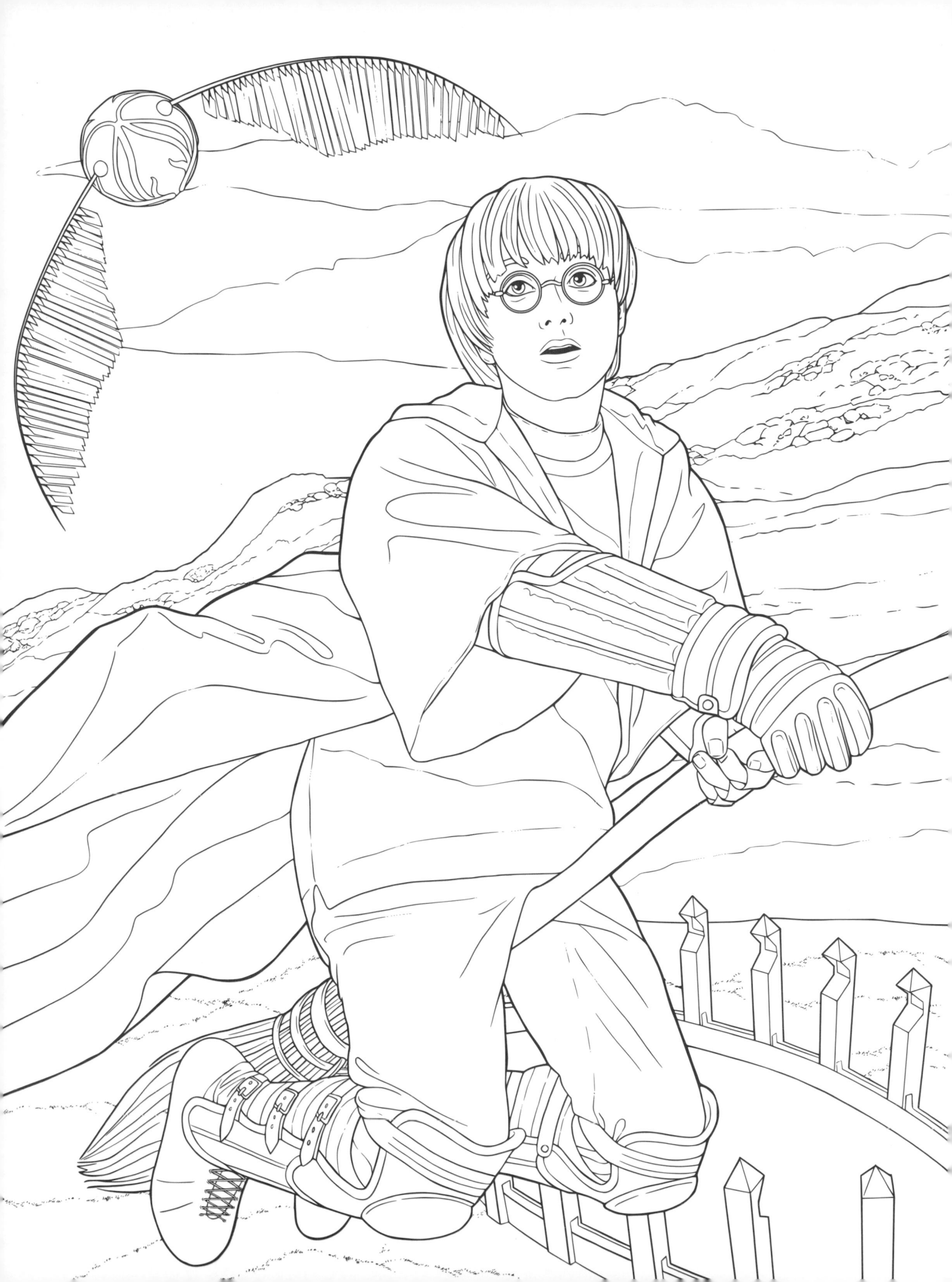

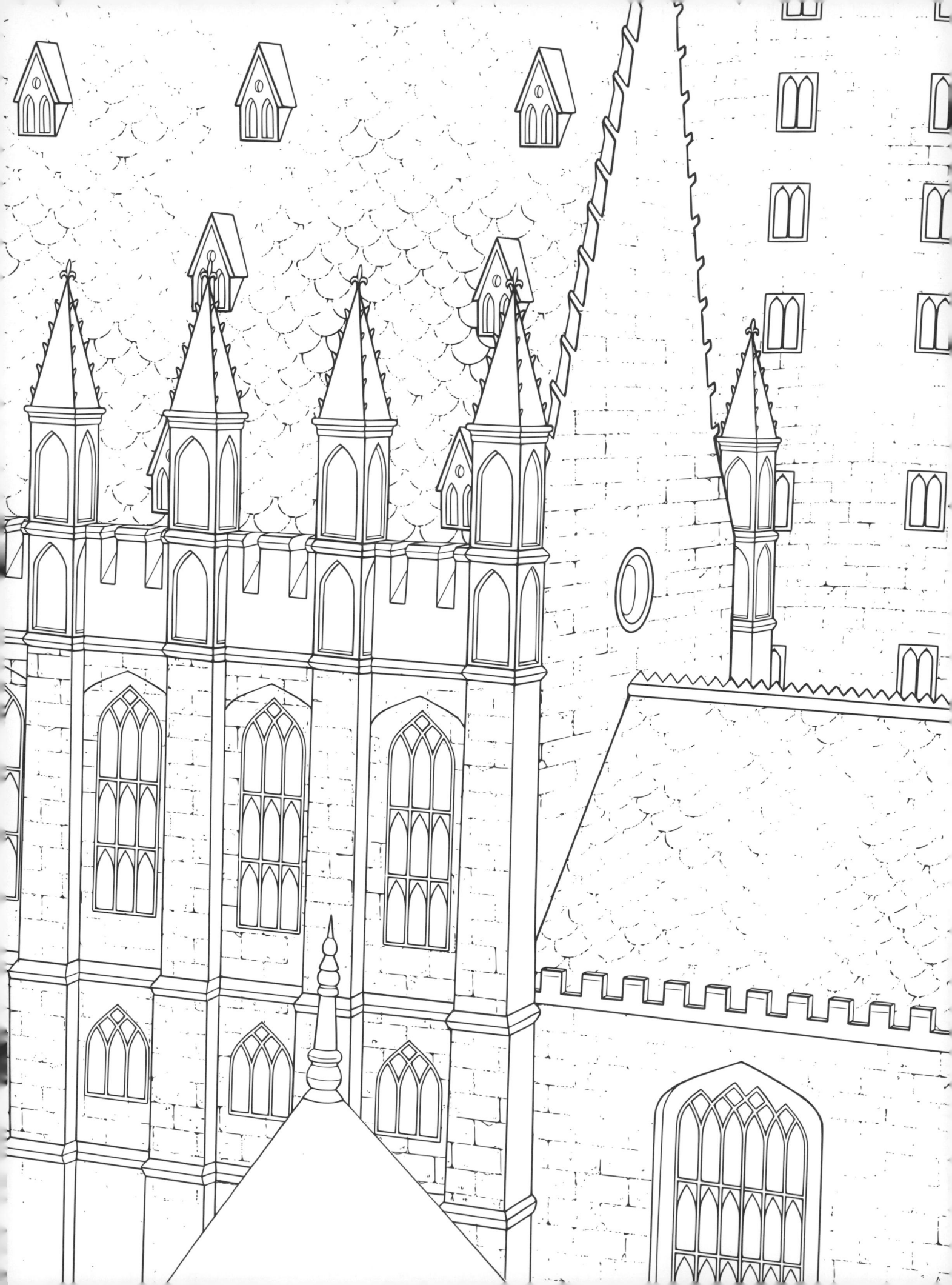

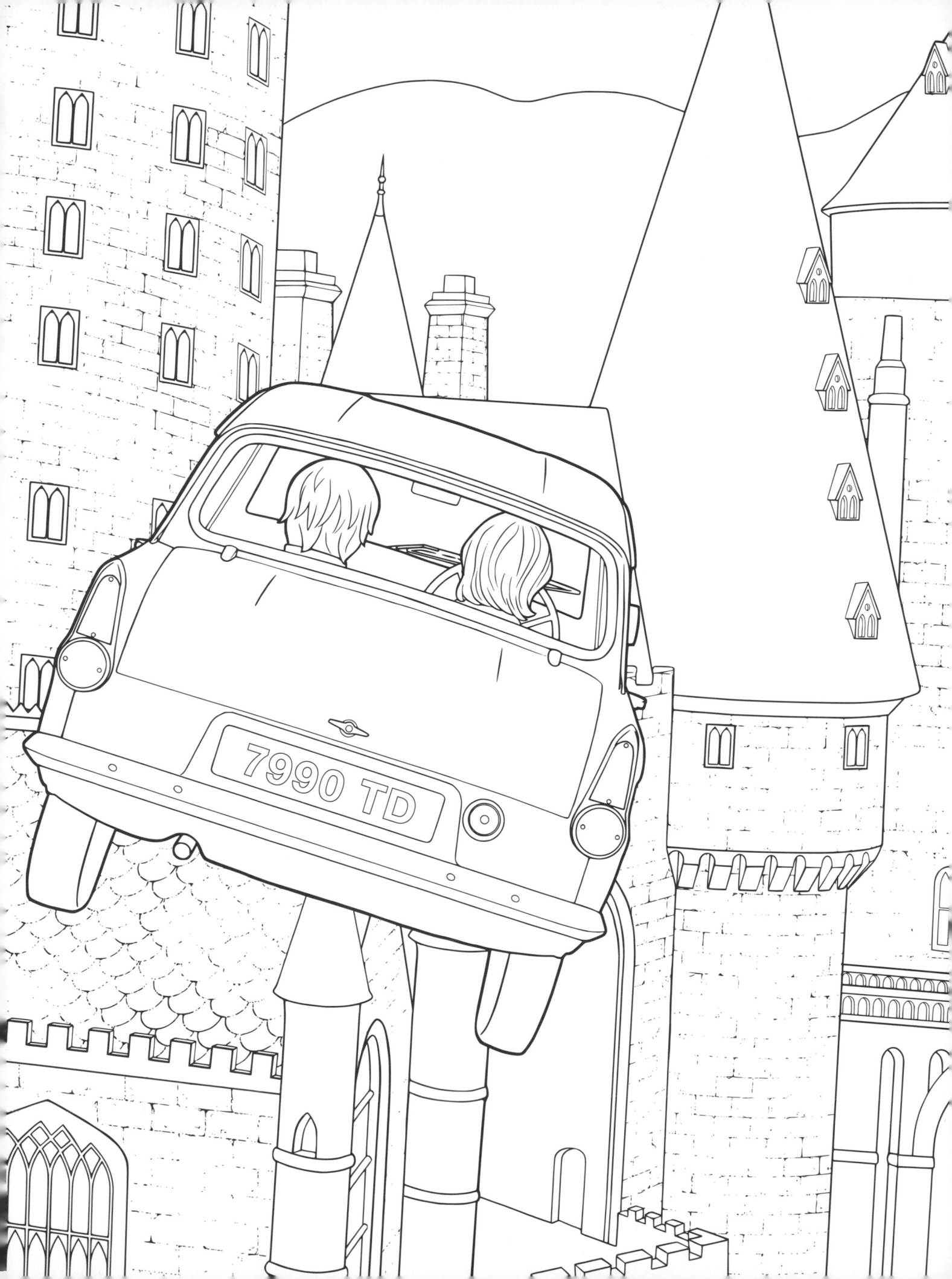
7990 TD

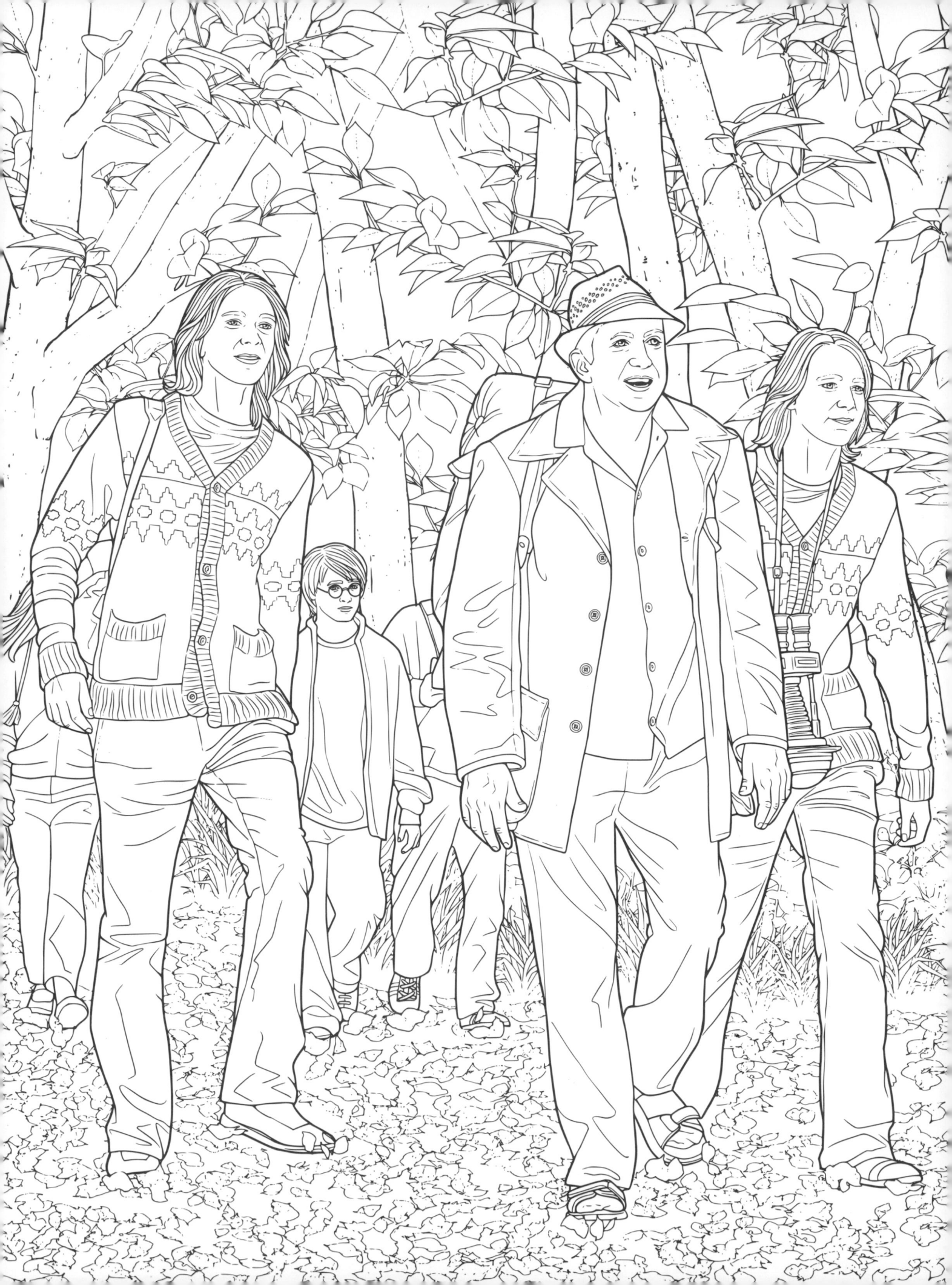

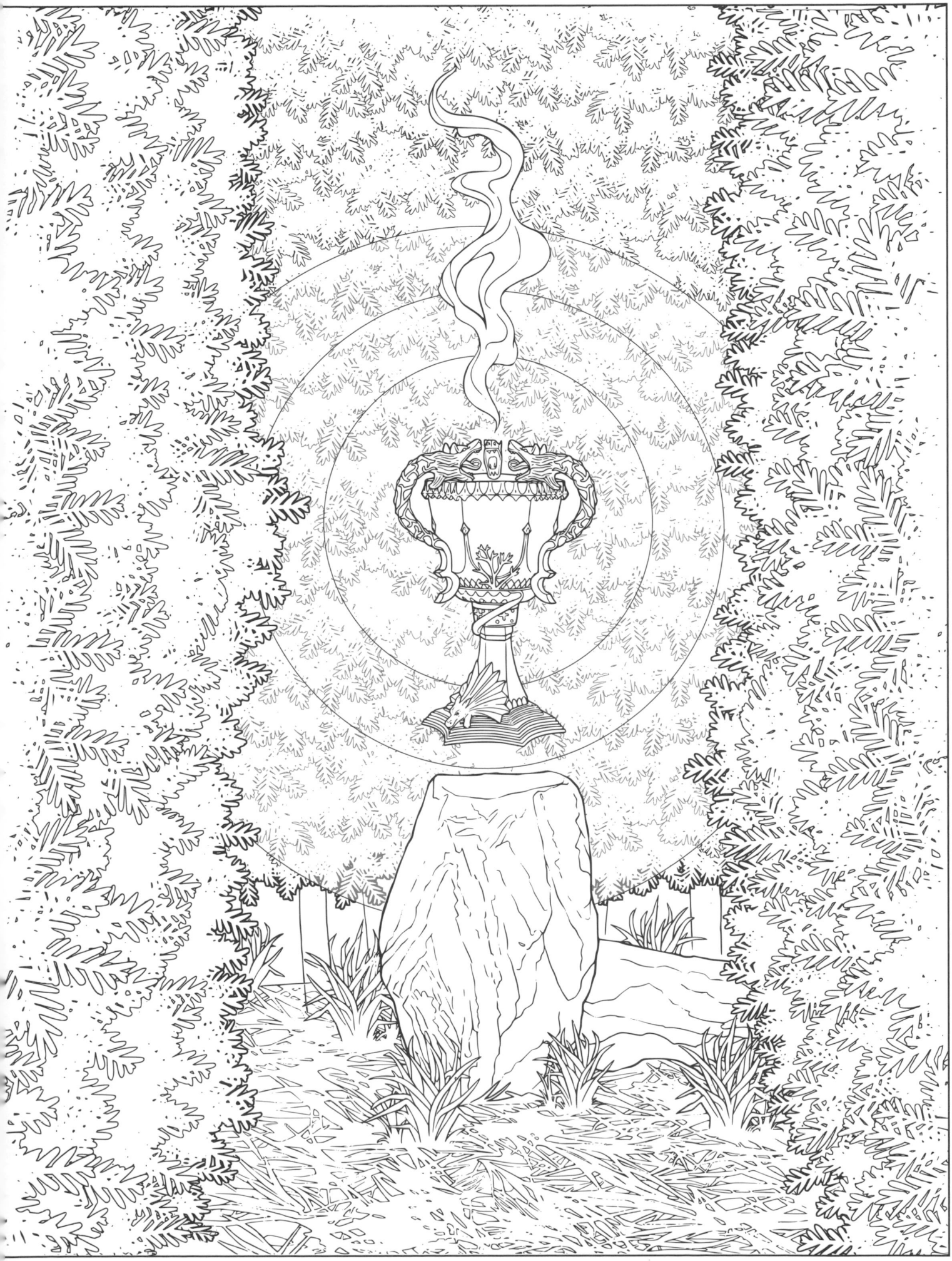

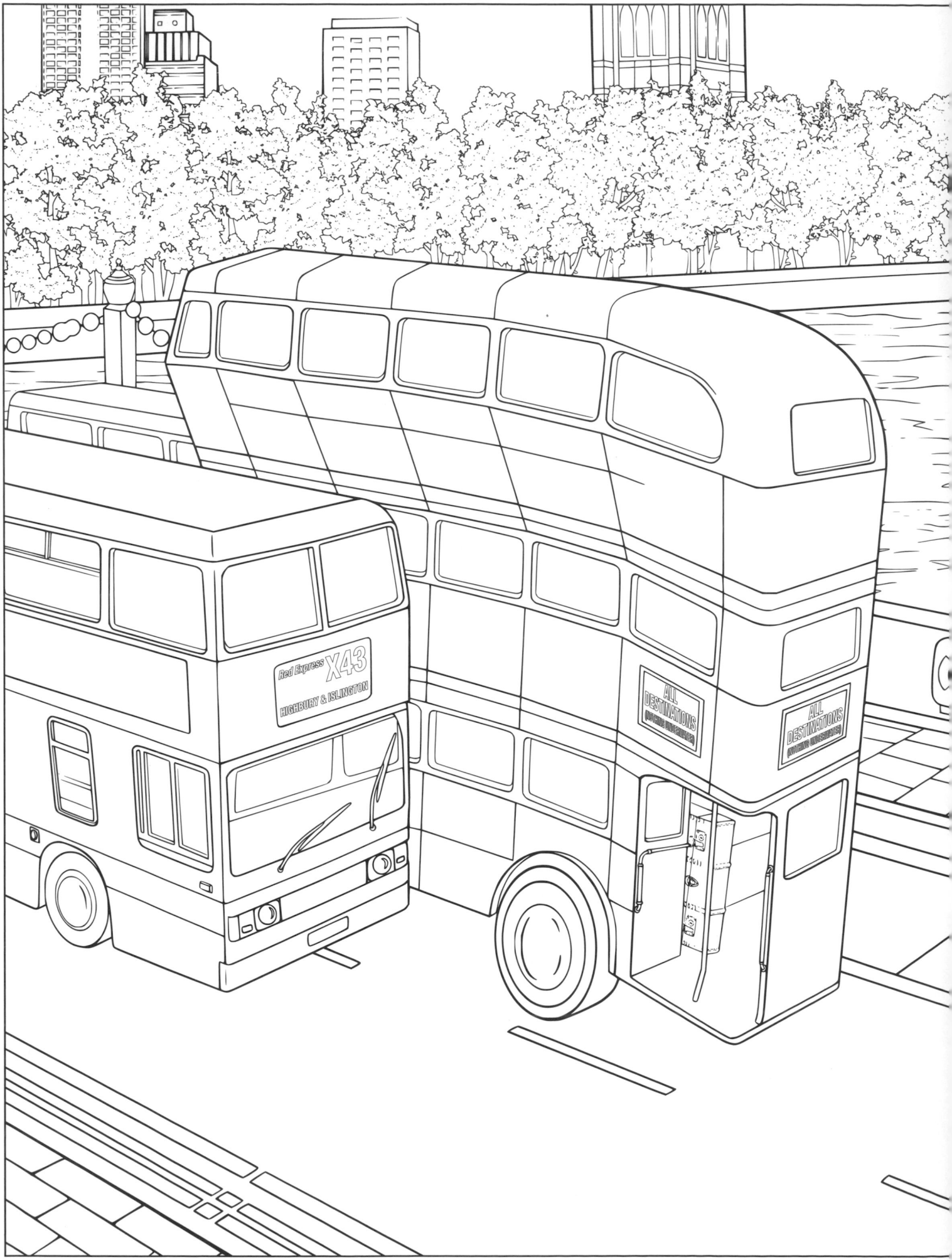
Red Express X43
HIGHBURY & ISLINGTON
ALL DESTINATIONS
ALL DESTINATIONS

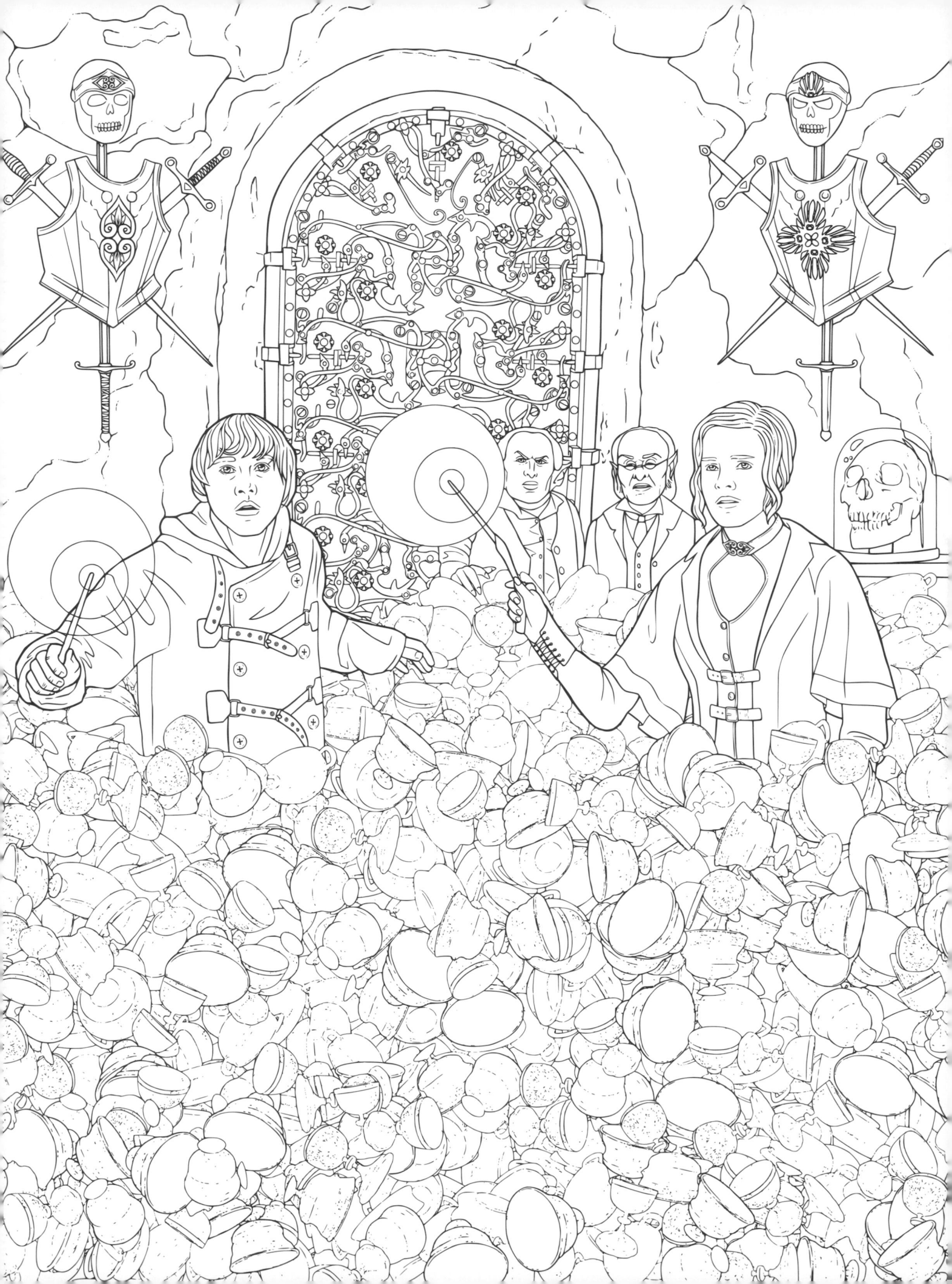

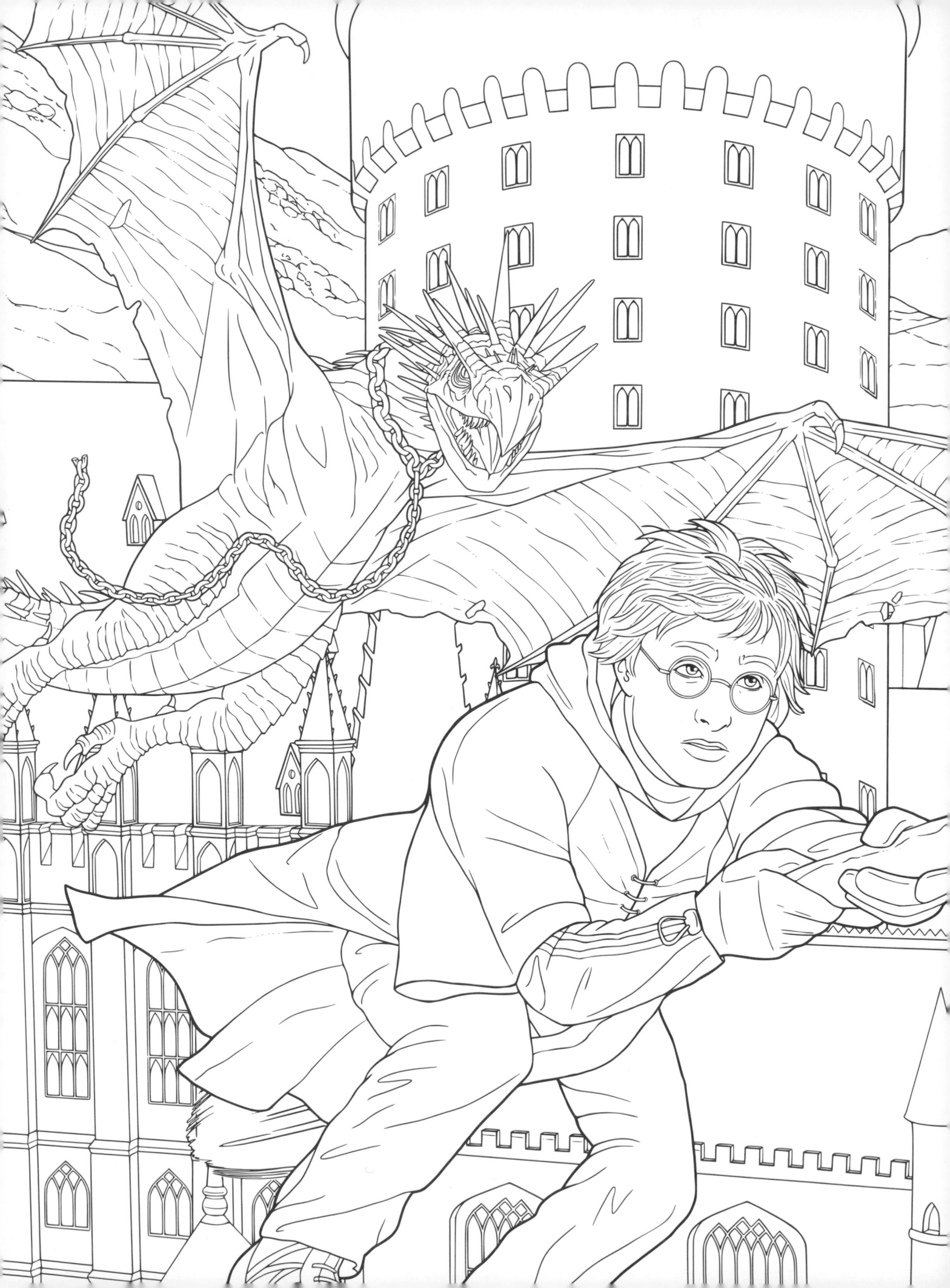

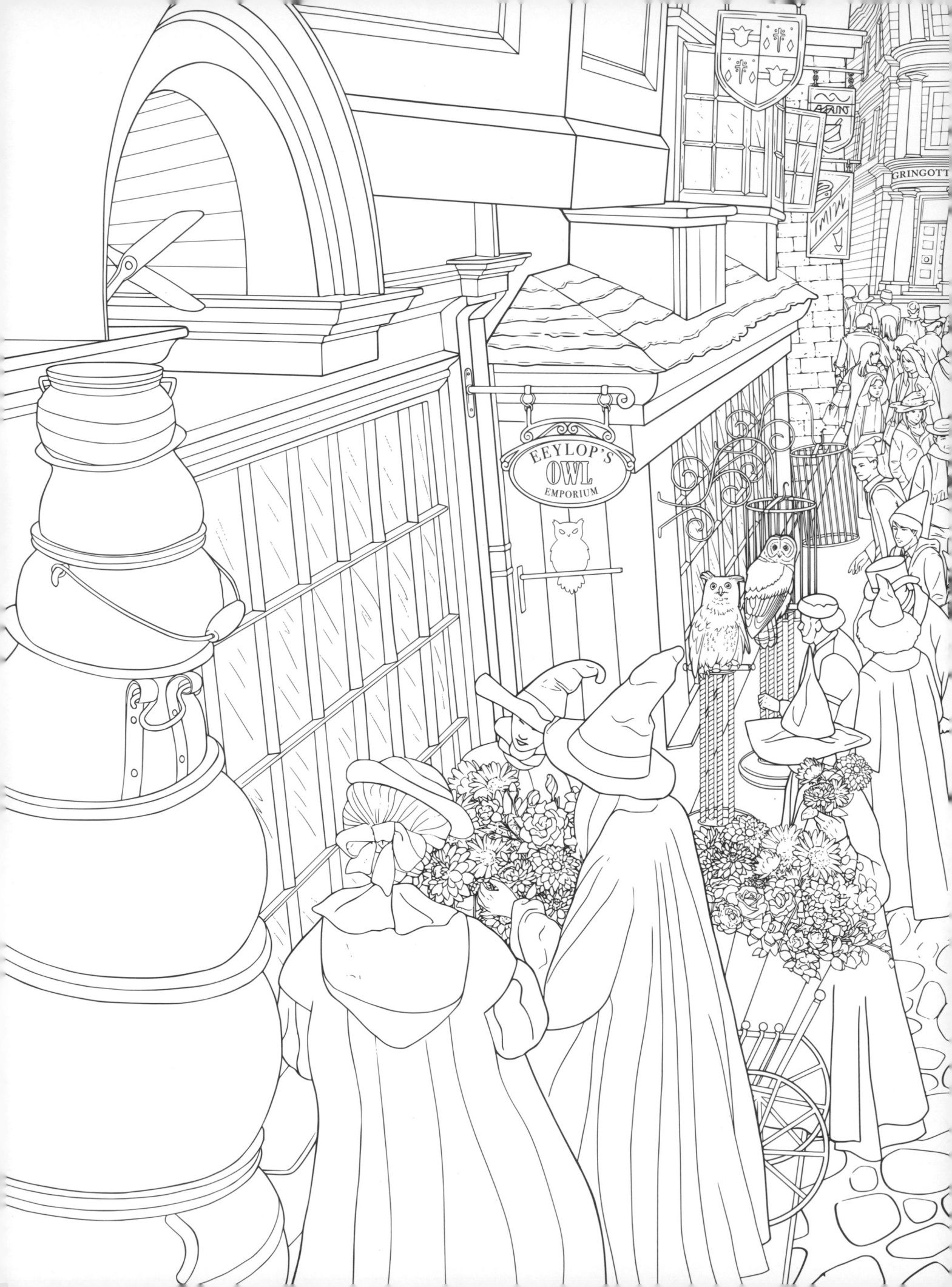
EEYLOP'S
OWL
EMPORIUM
GRINGOTT

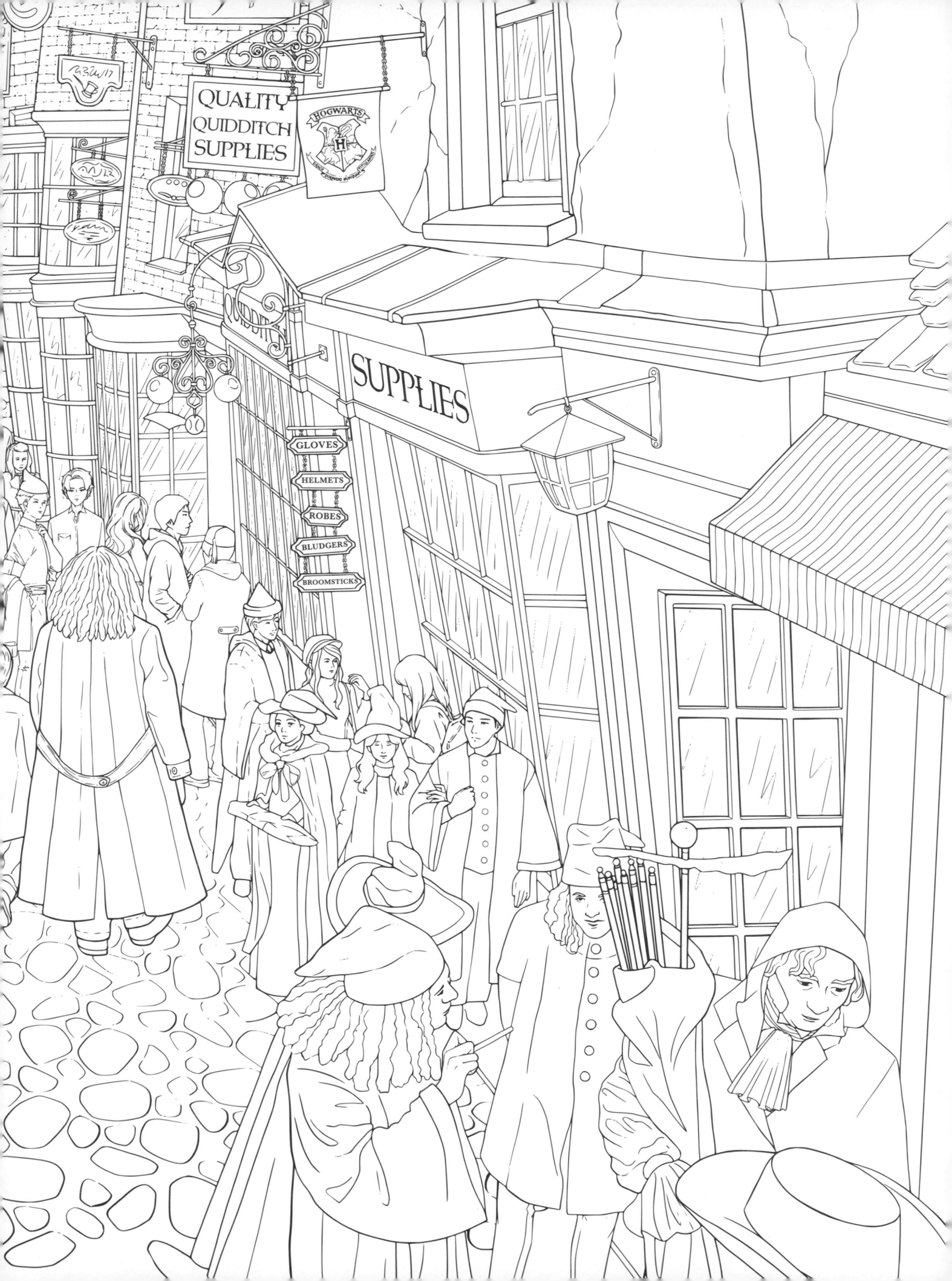
QUALITY
QUIDDITCH
SUPPLIES
HOGWARTS
QUIDDITCH
SUPPLIES
GLOVES
HELMETS
ROBES
BLUDGERS
BROOMSTICKS

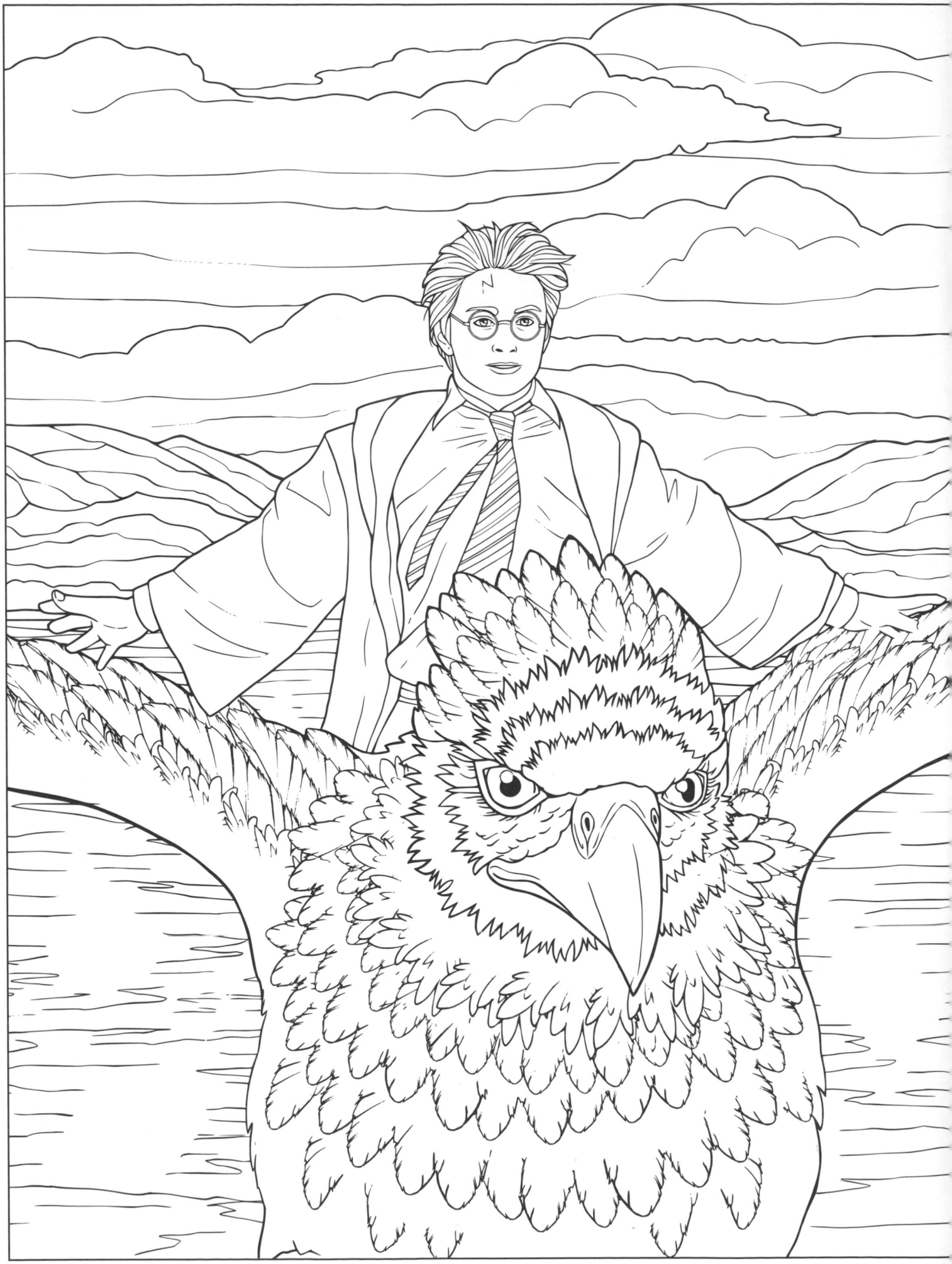

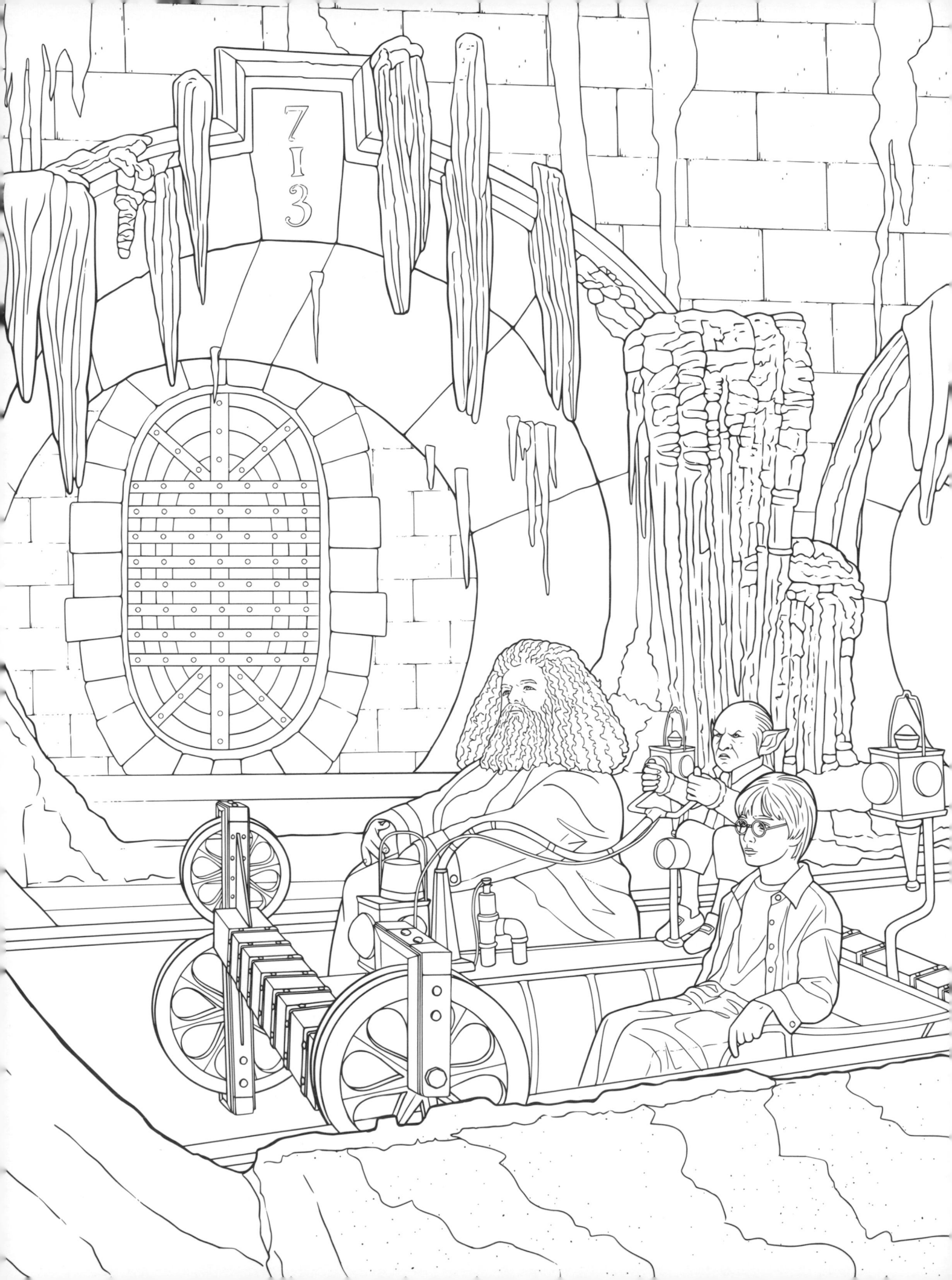
713

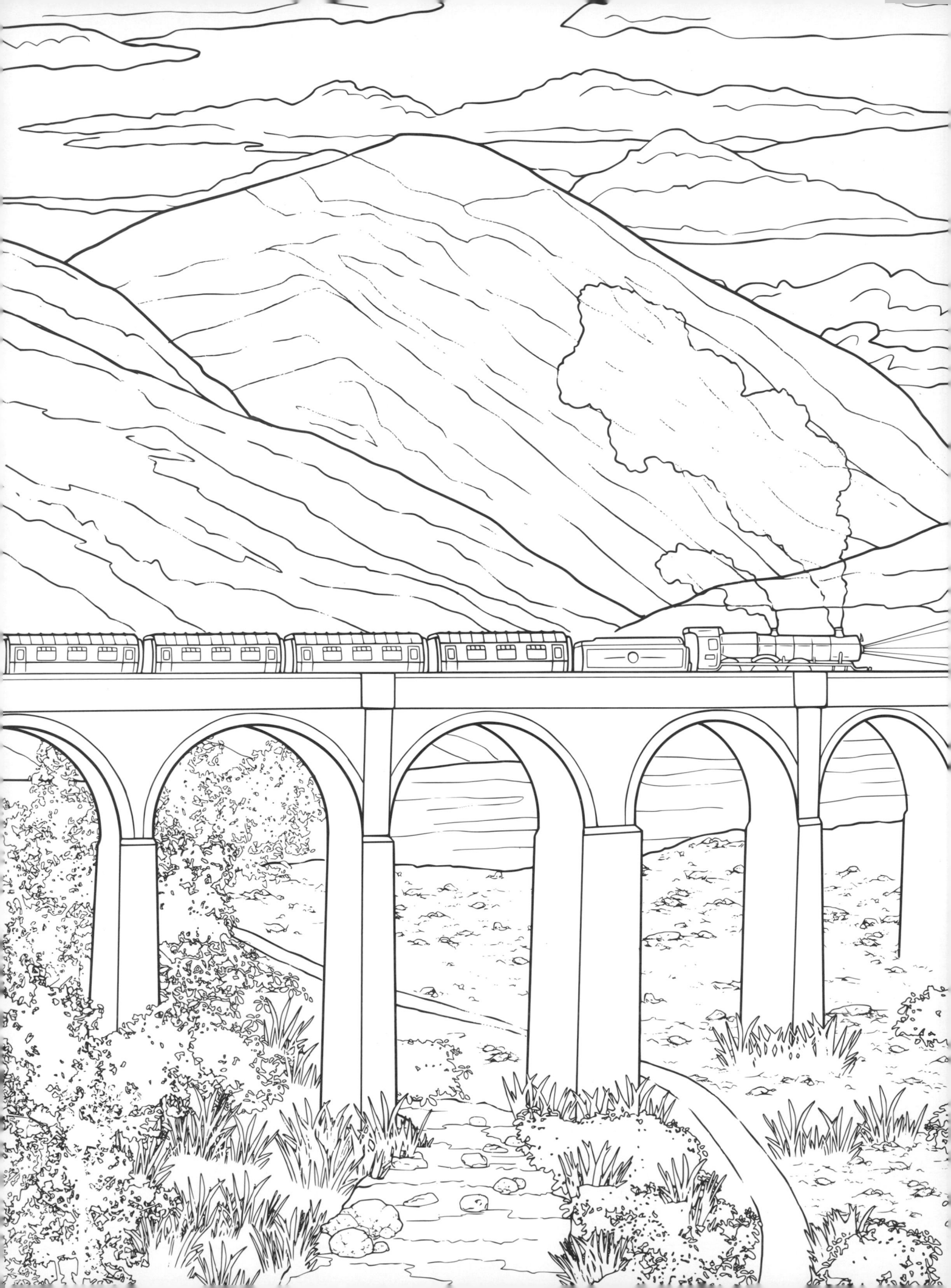

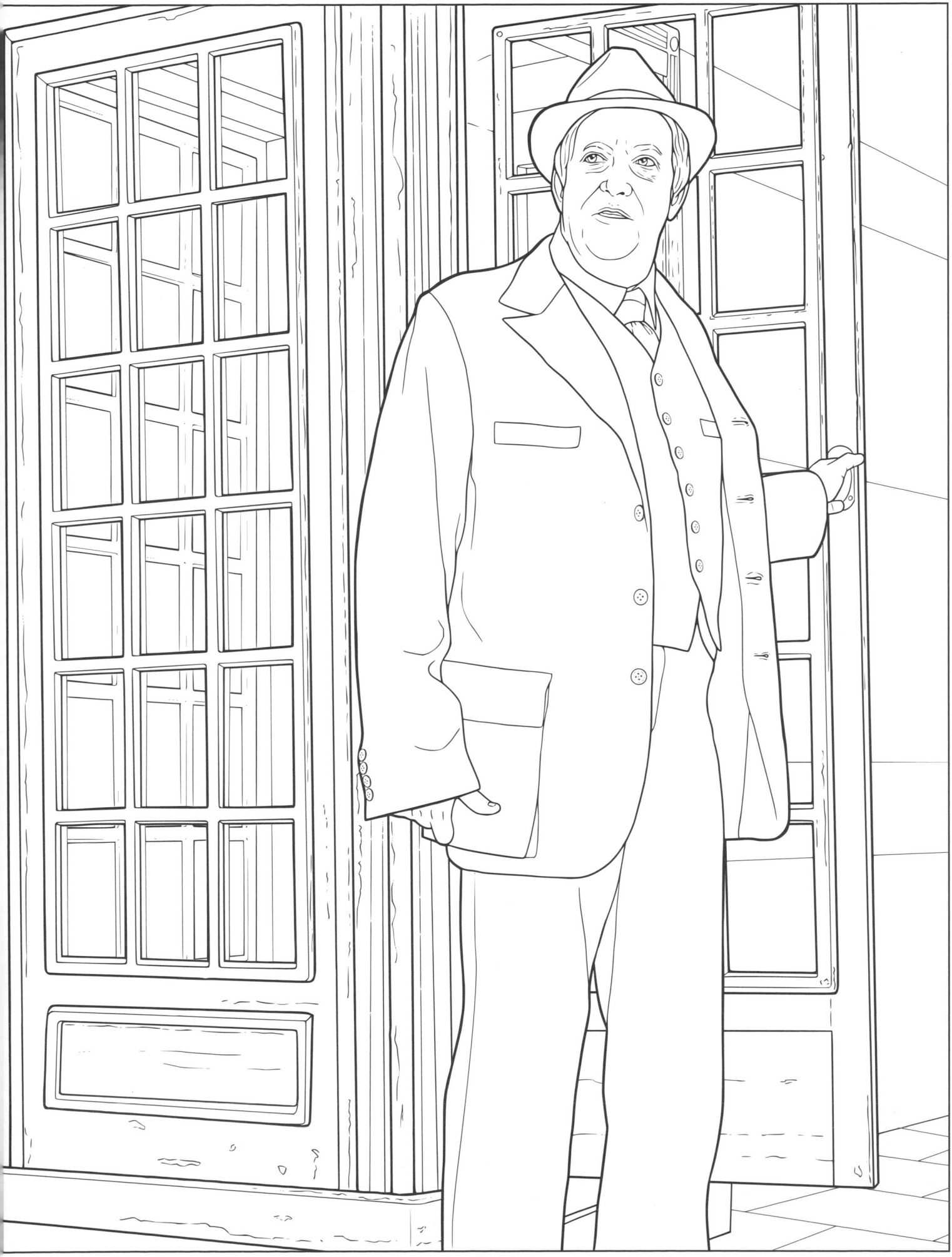

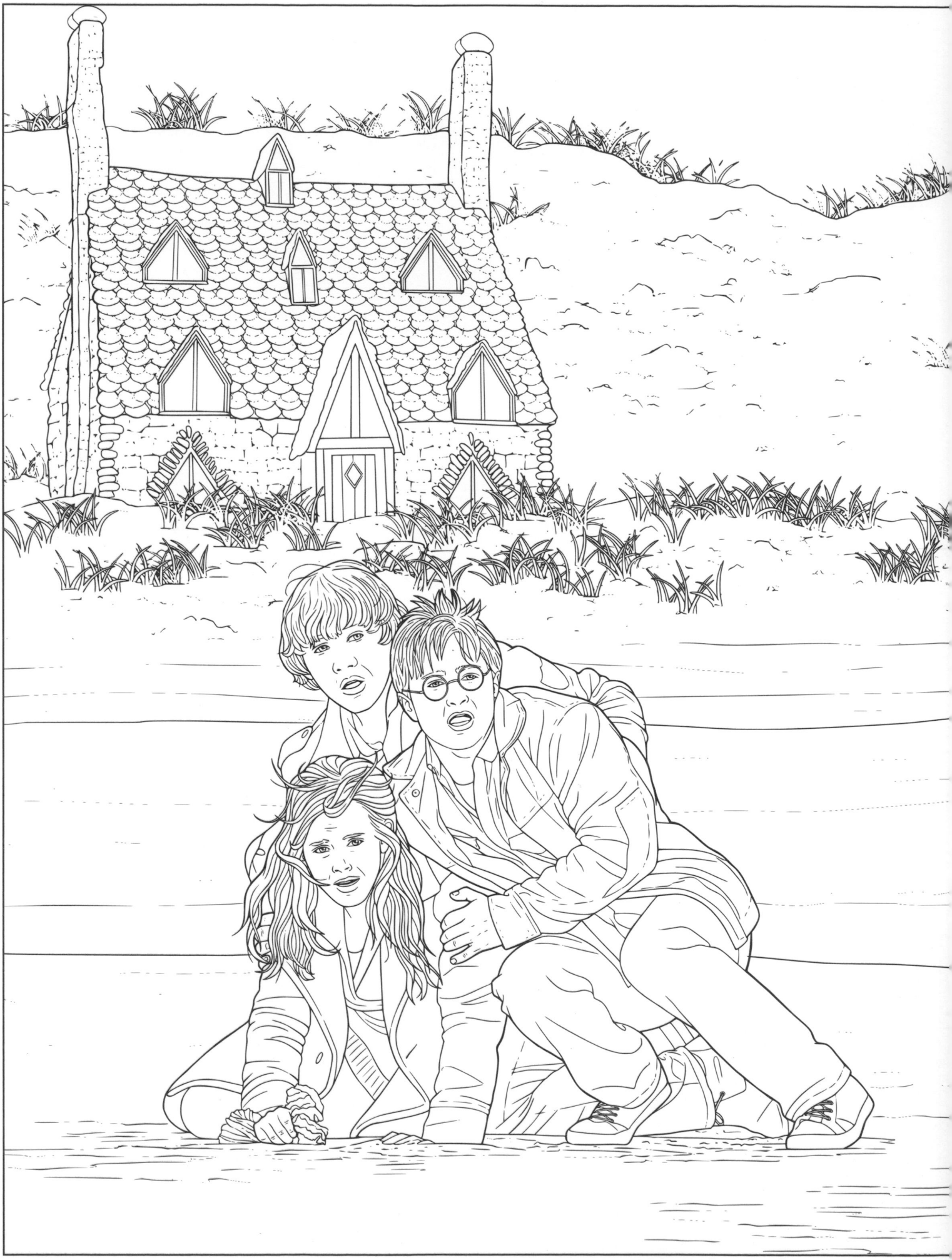

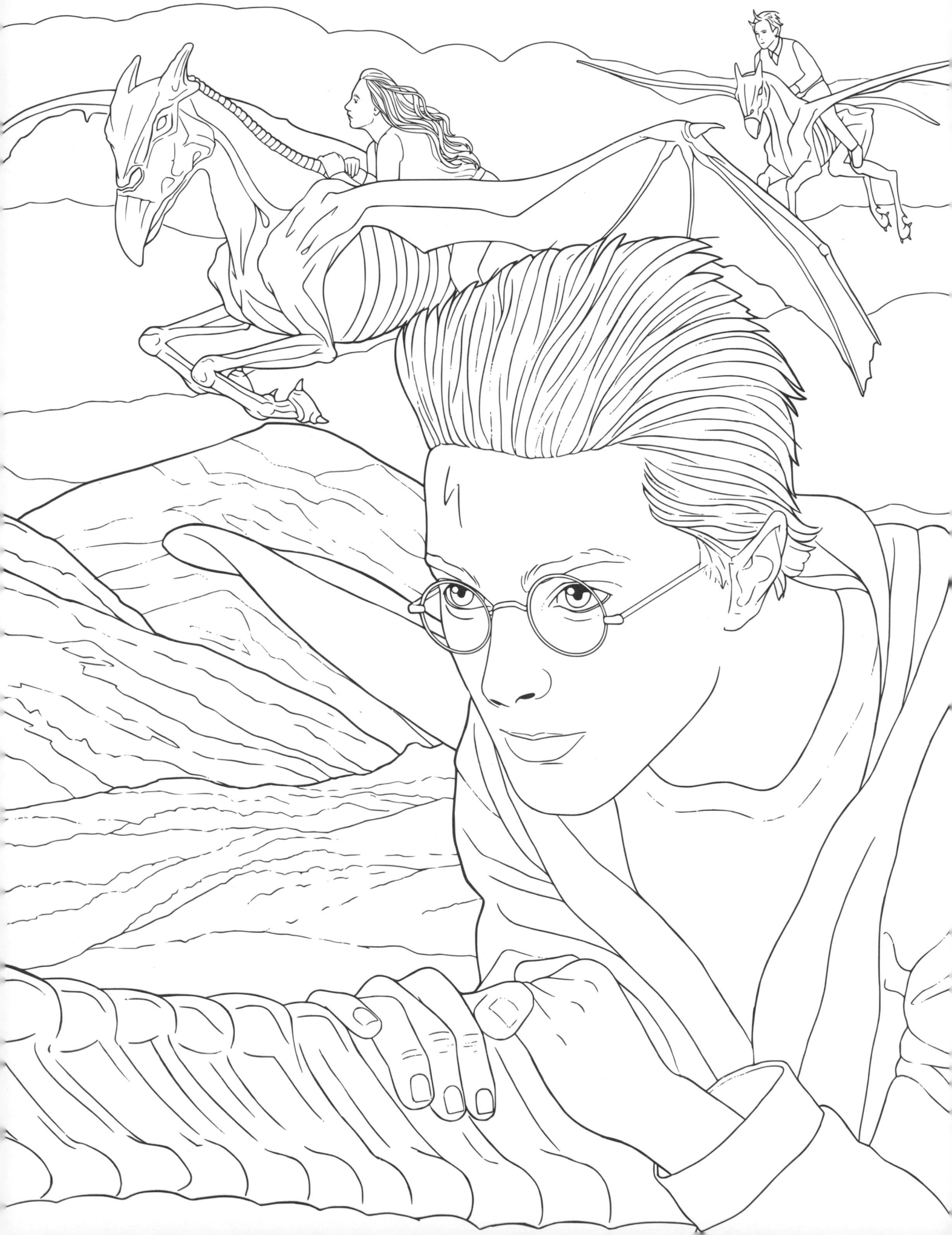

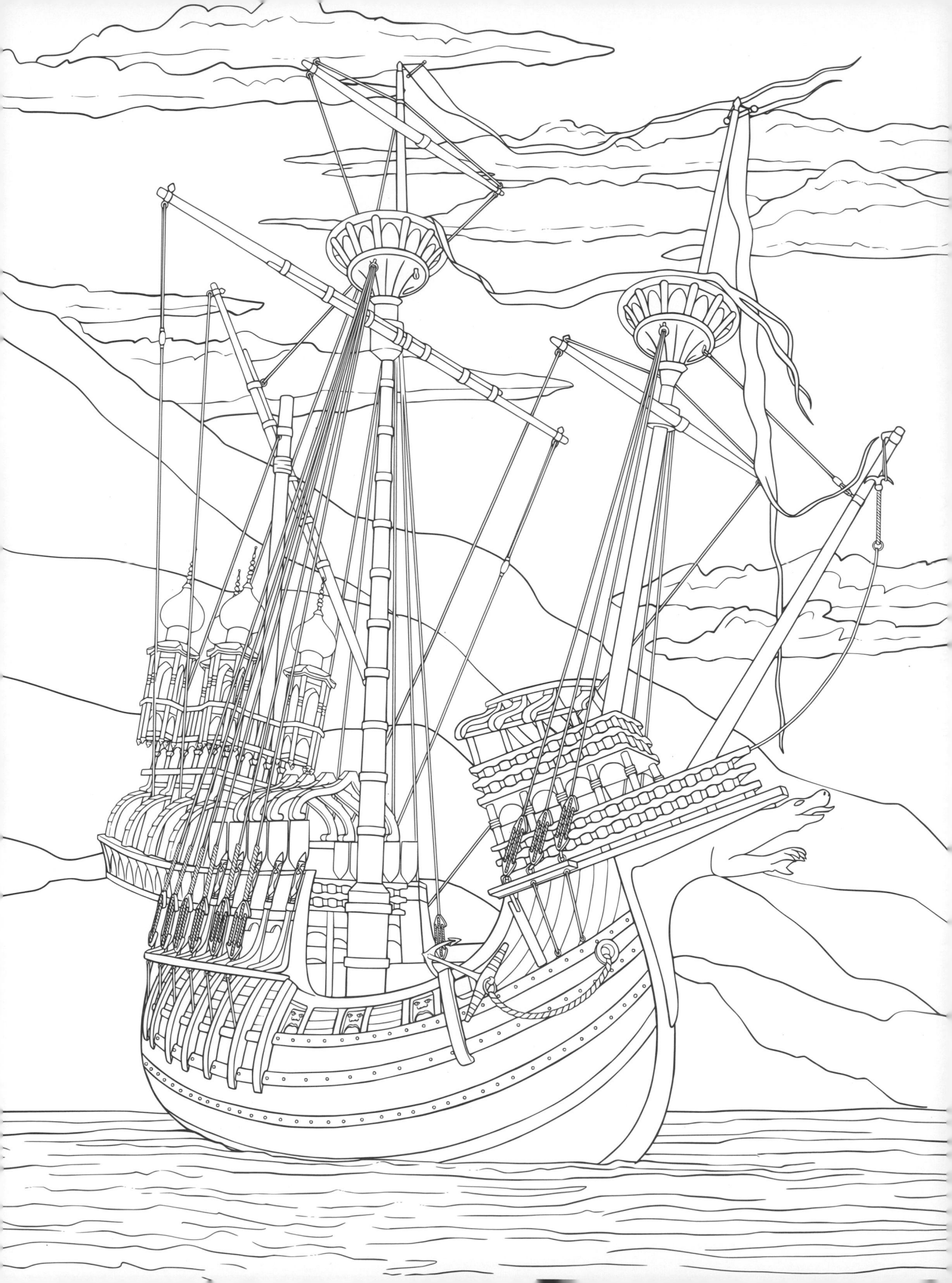

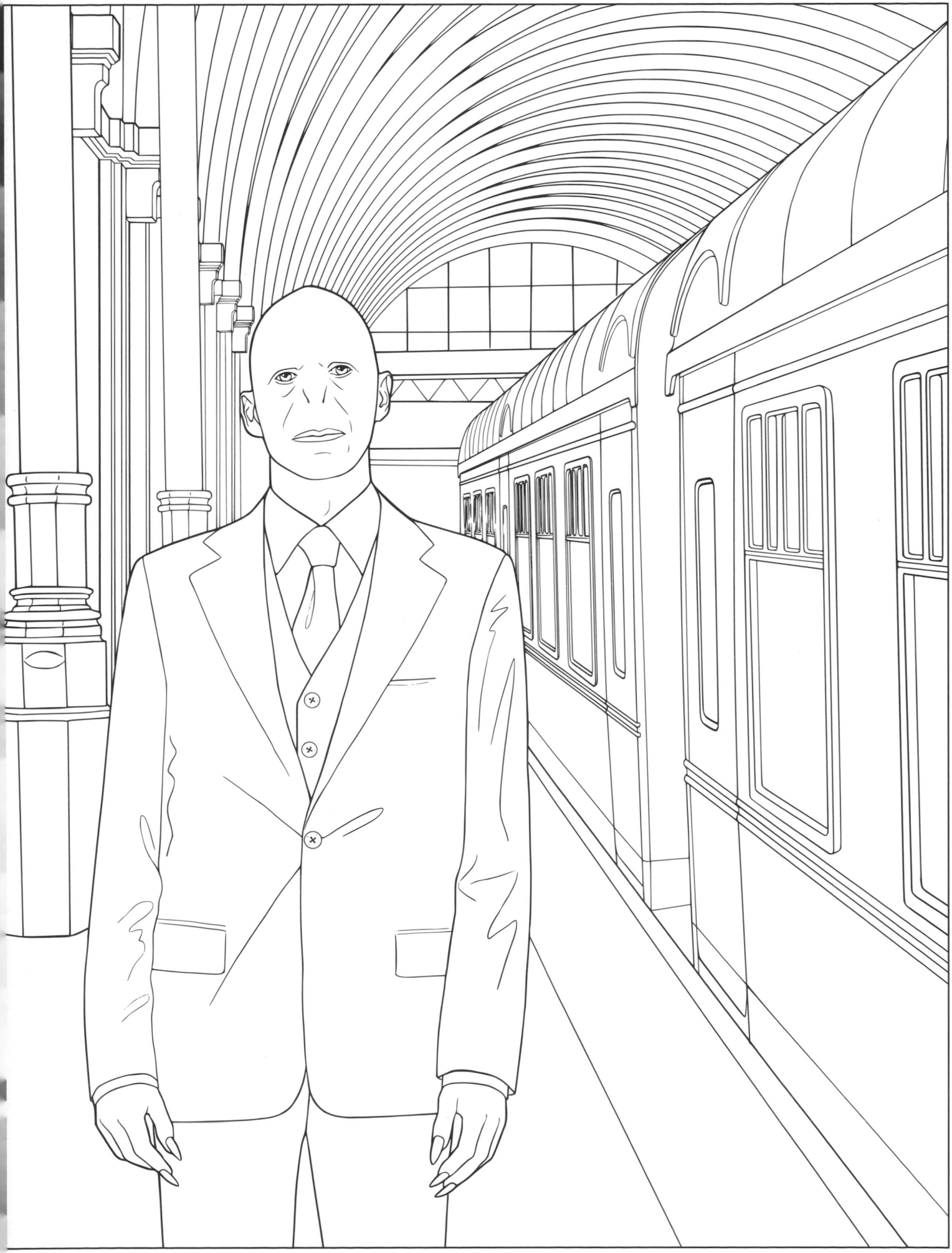

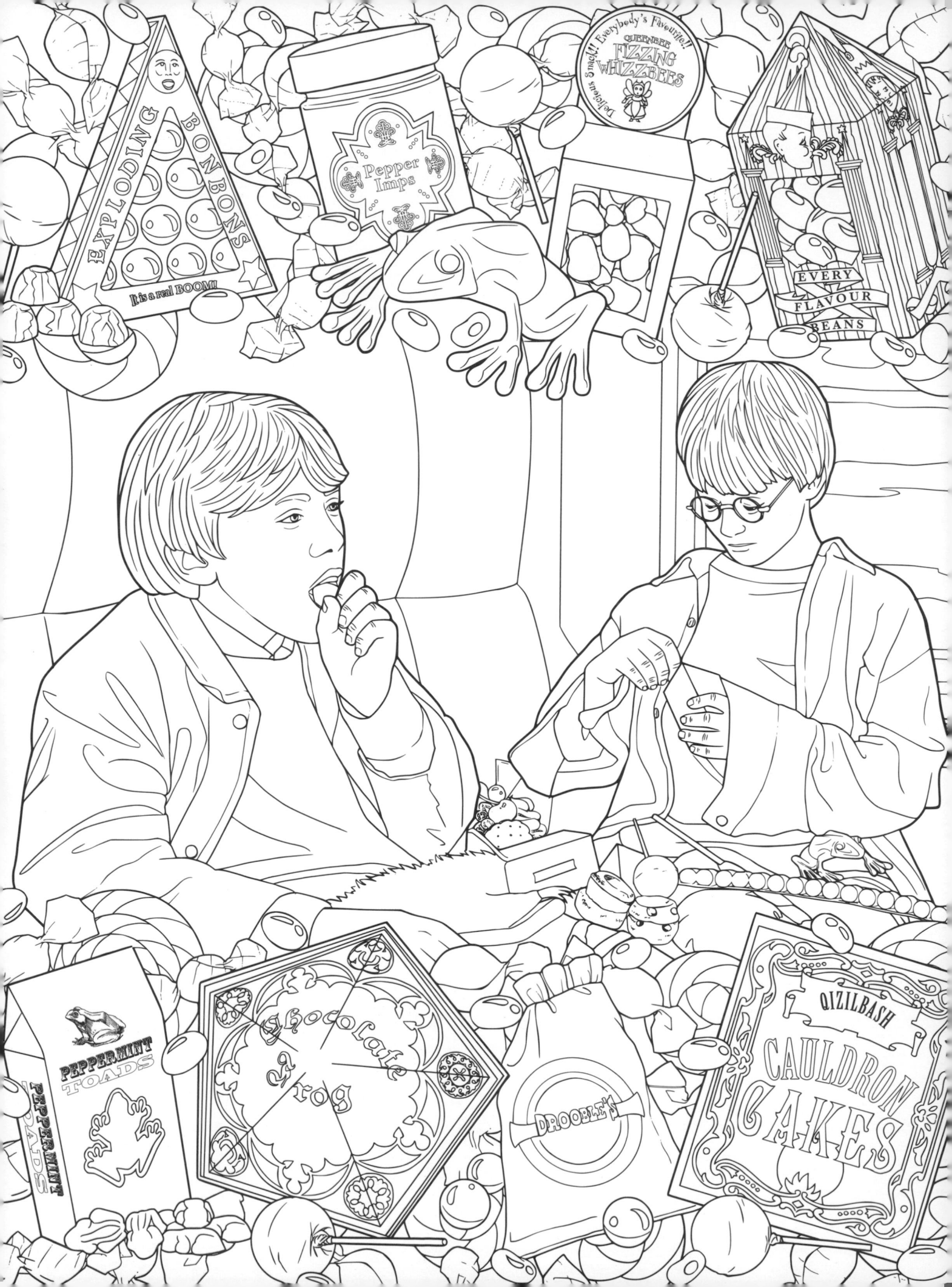
EXPLODING BONBONS
It is a real BOOM!
Pepper Imps
Delicious Snack!! Everybody's Favourite!!
QUERNBEE
FIZZING WHIZZBEES
EVERY FLAVOUR BEANS
PEPPERMINT TOADS
Chocolate Frog
DROOBLE'S
QIZILBASH
CAULDRON CAKES

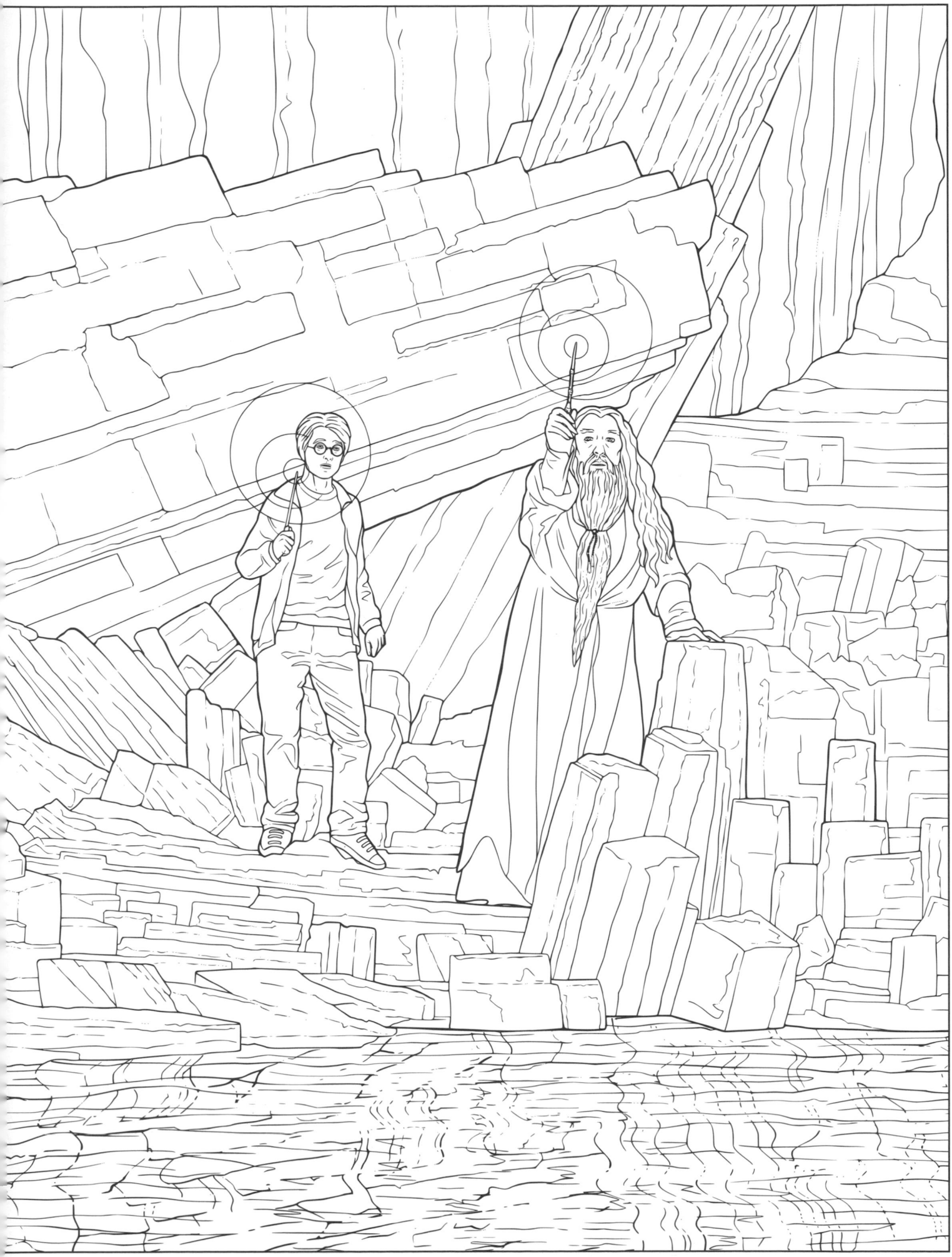

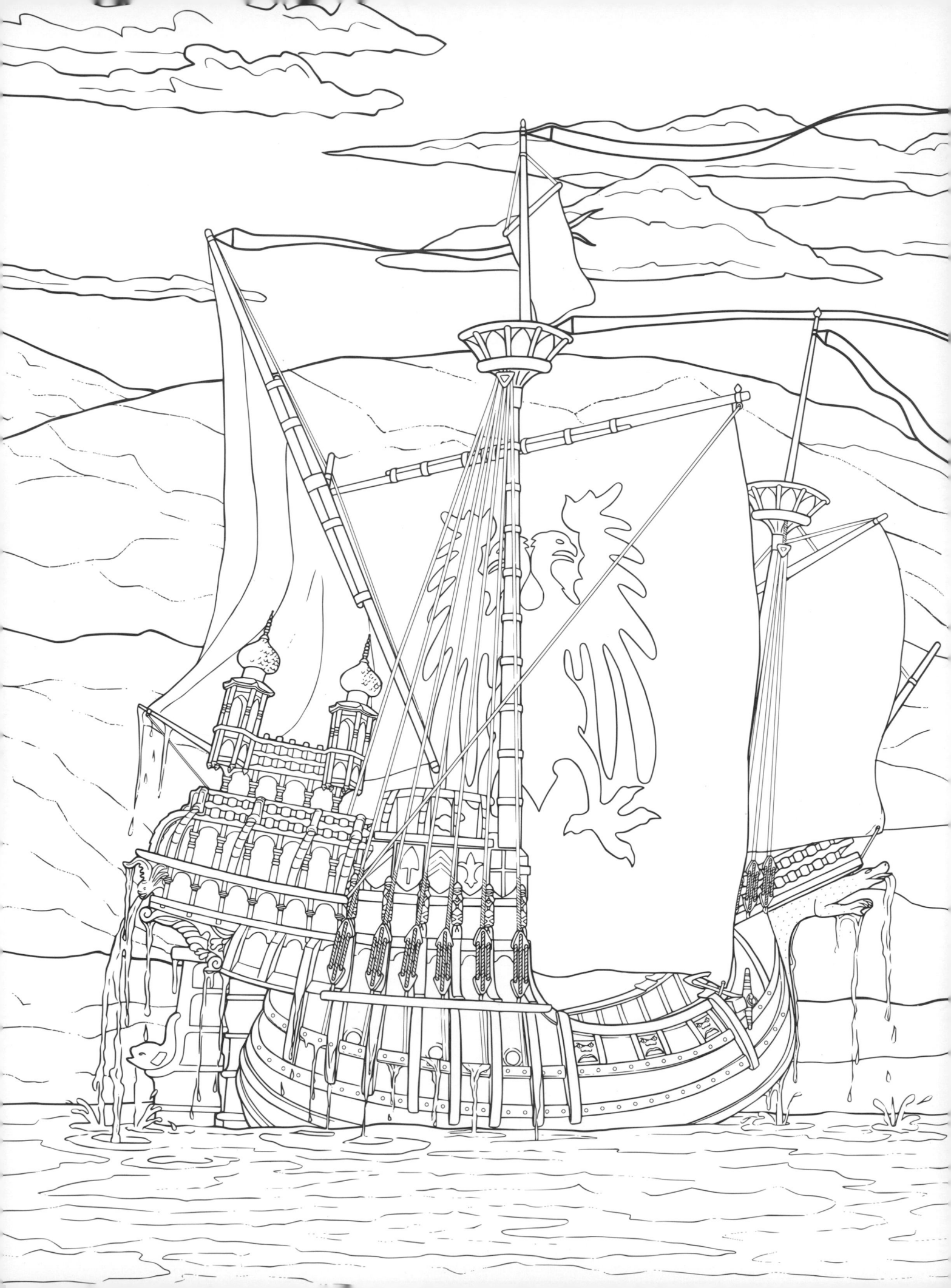

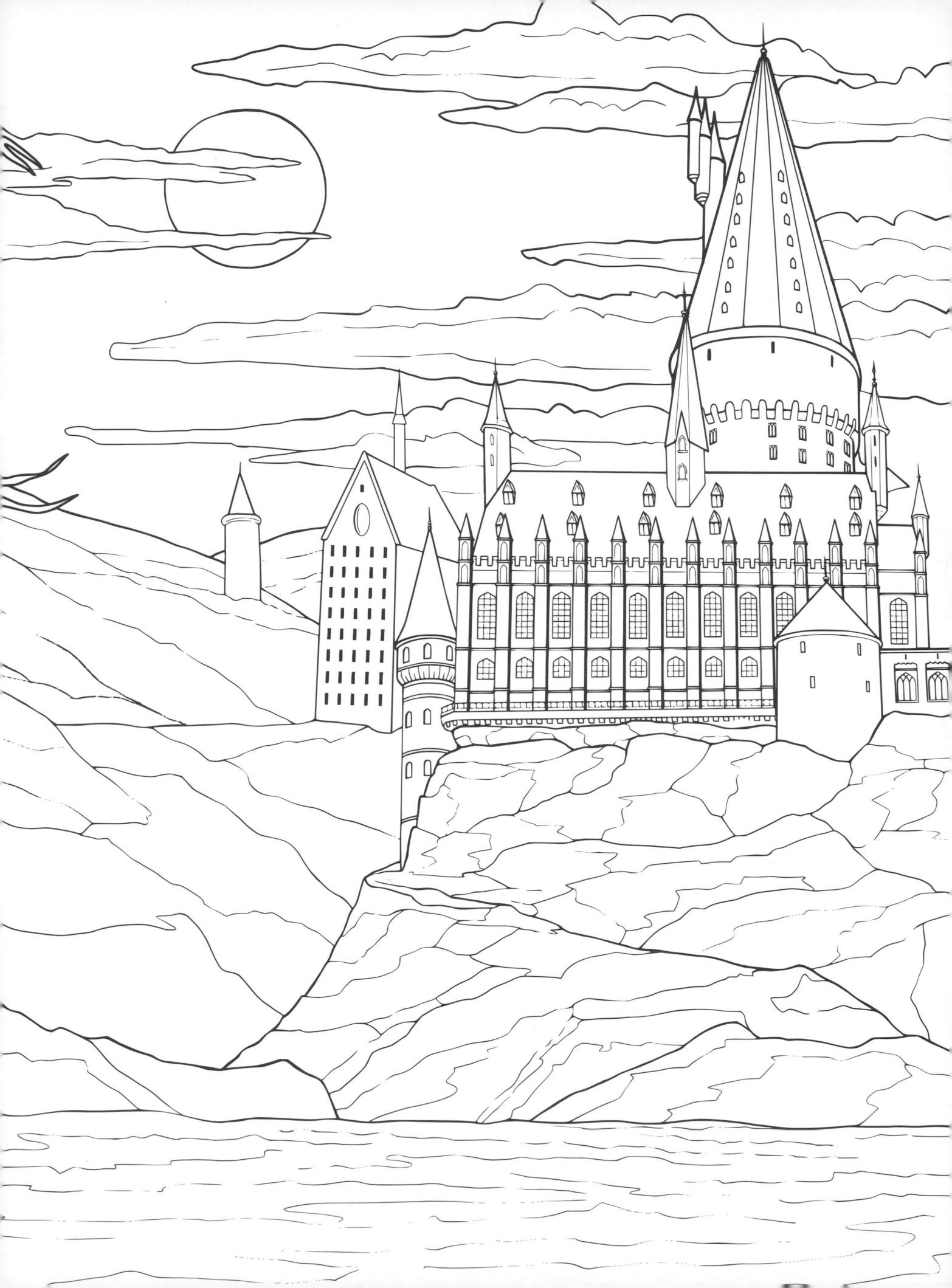

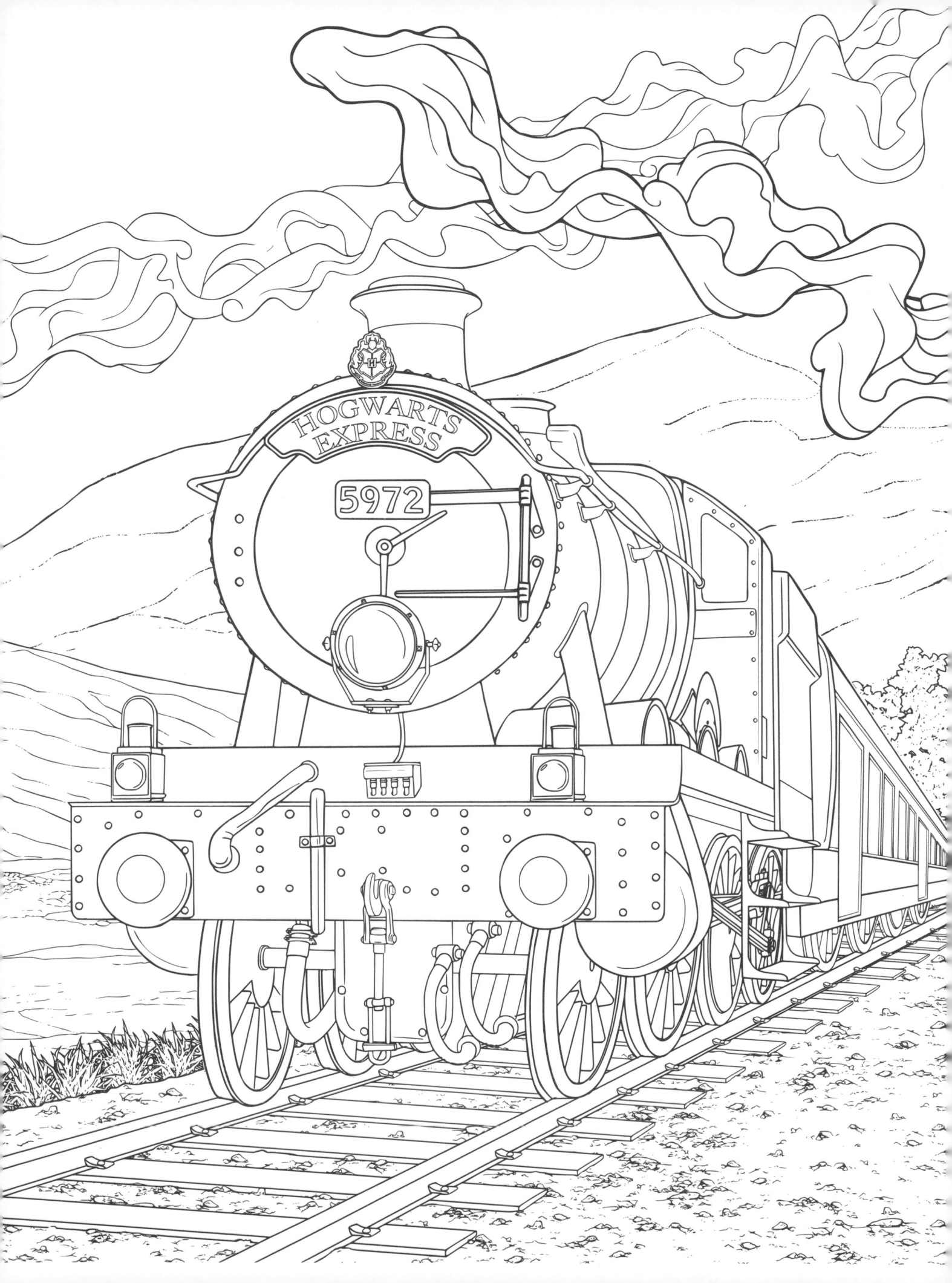
HOGWARTS
EXPRESS
5972

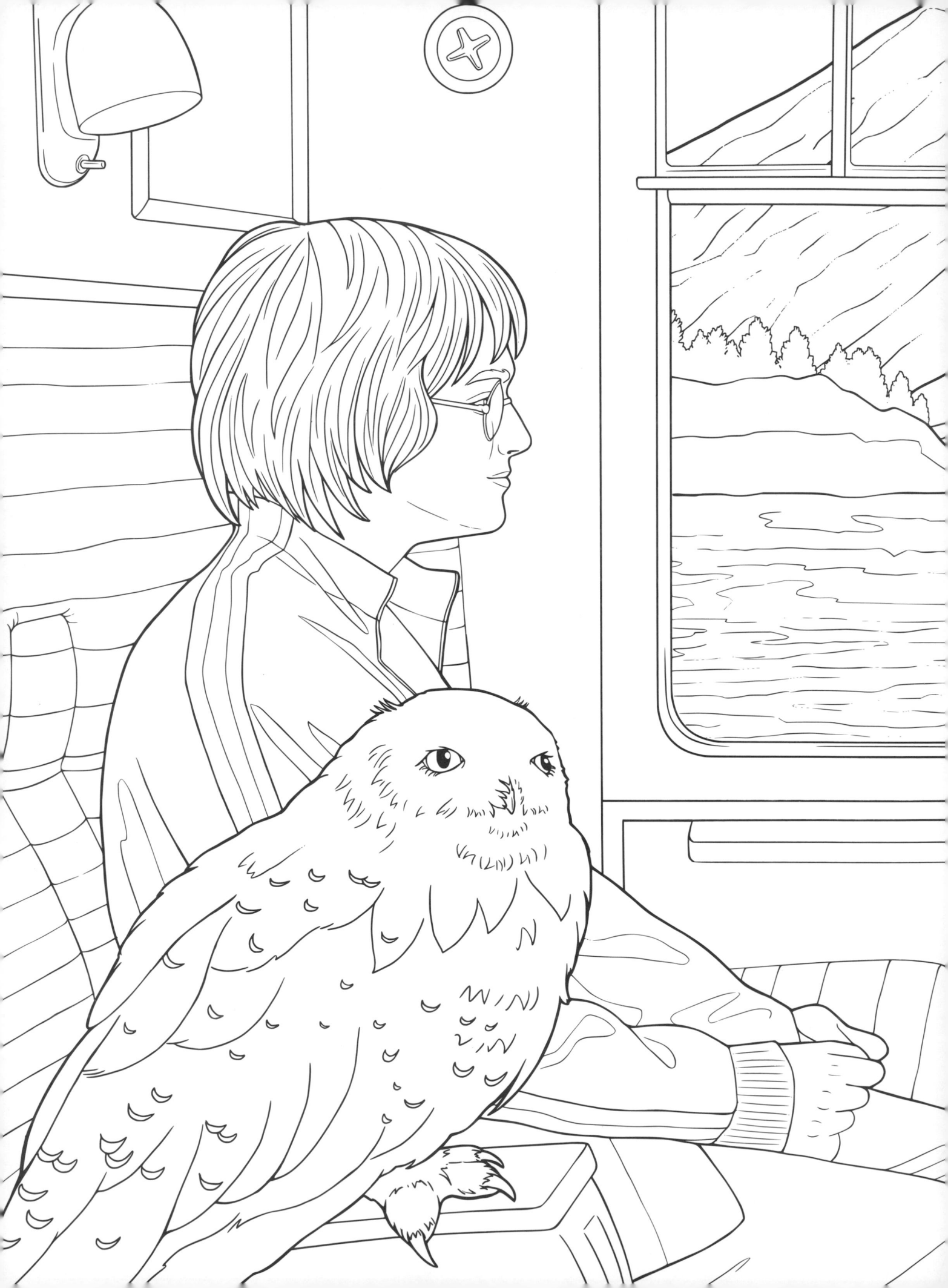

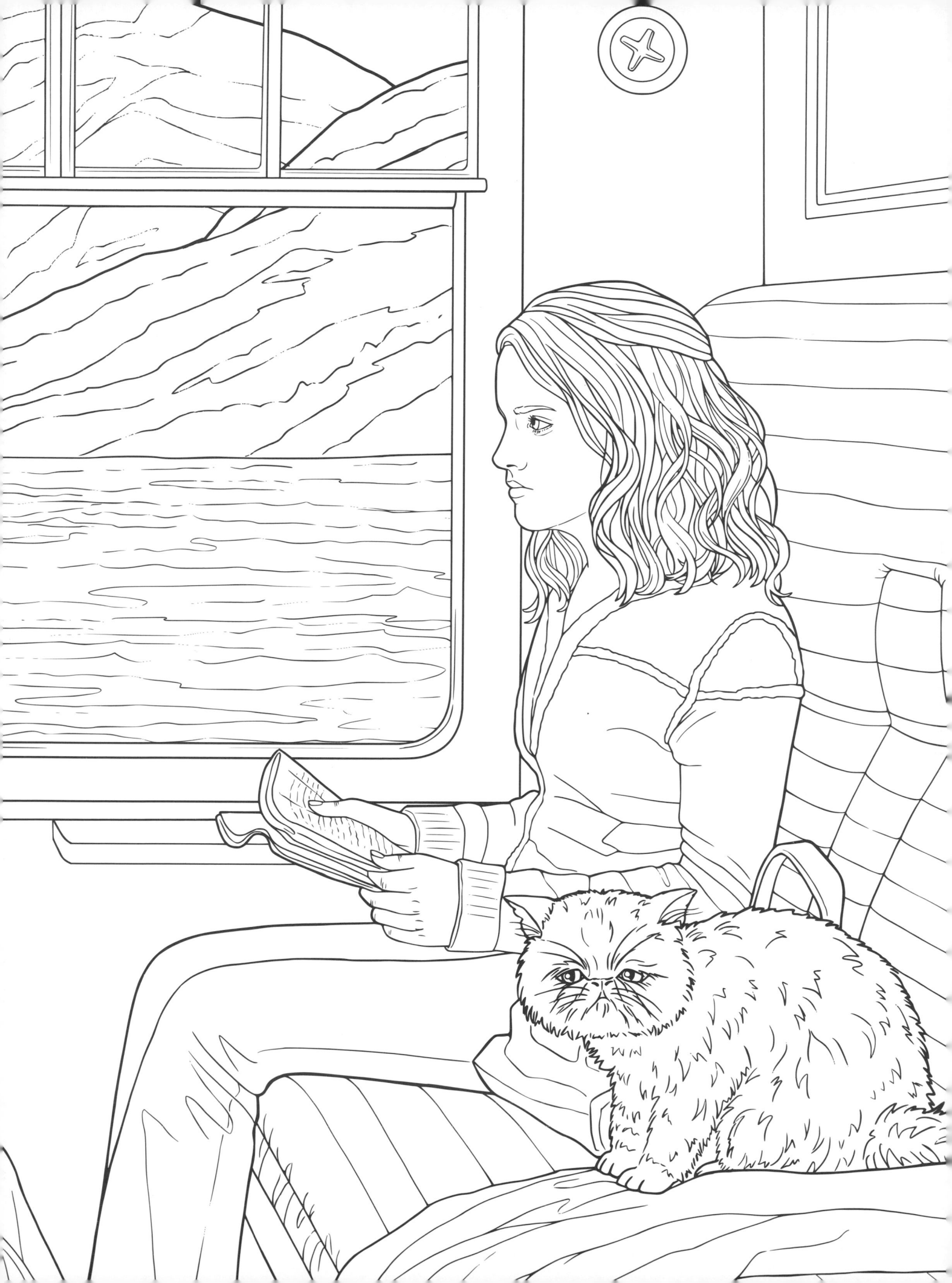

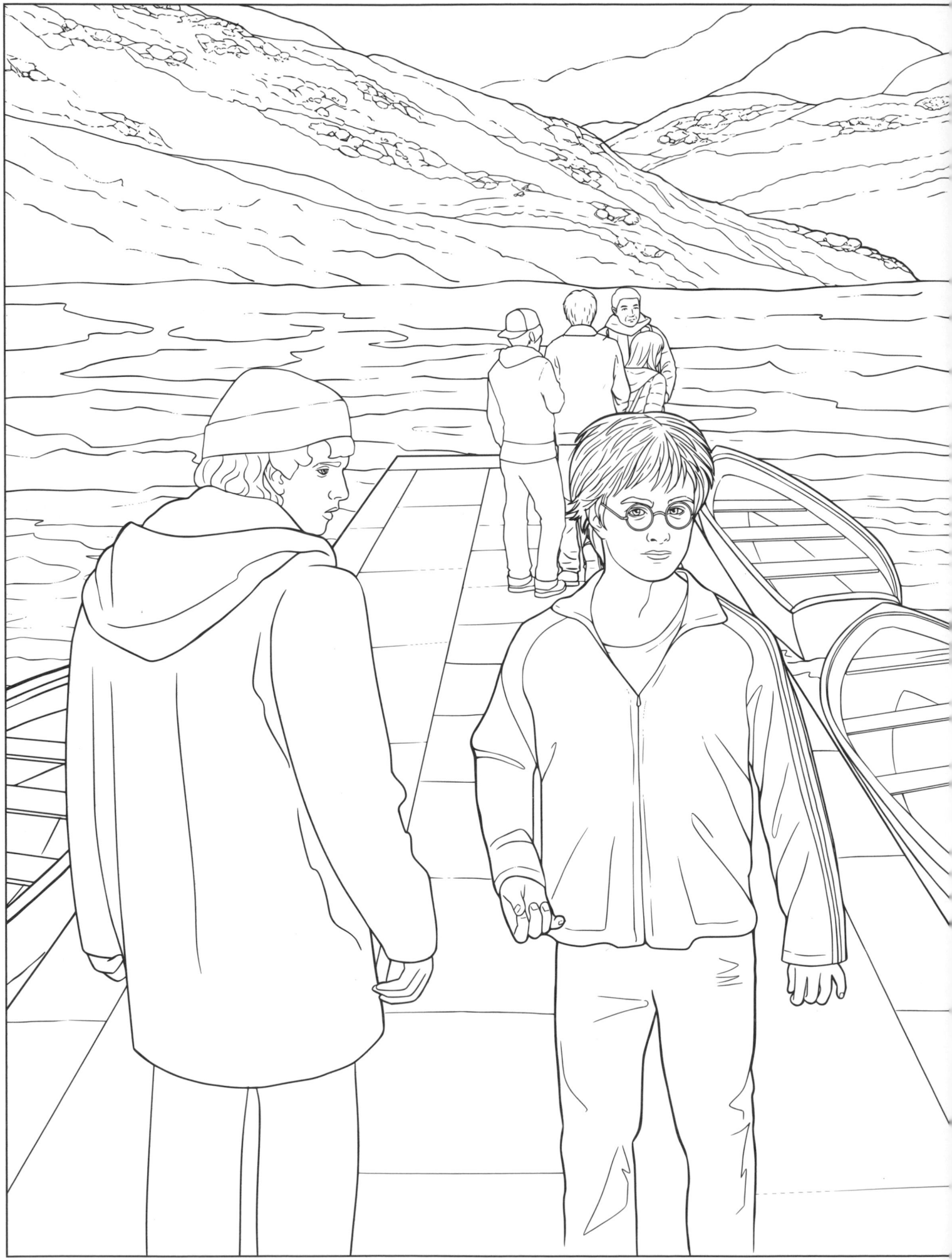

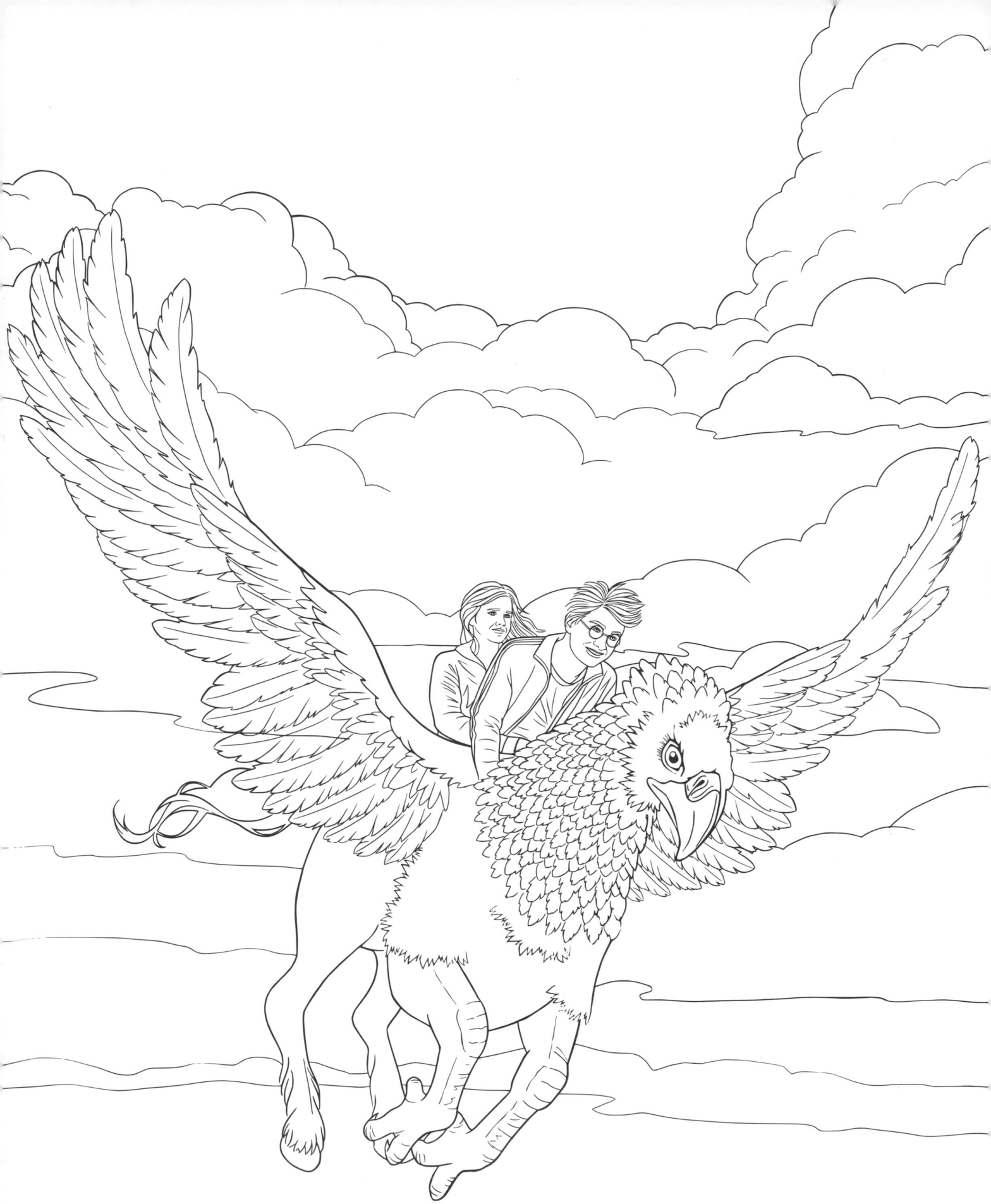

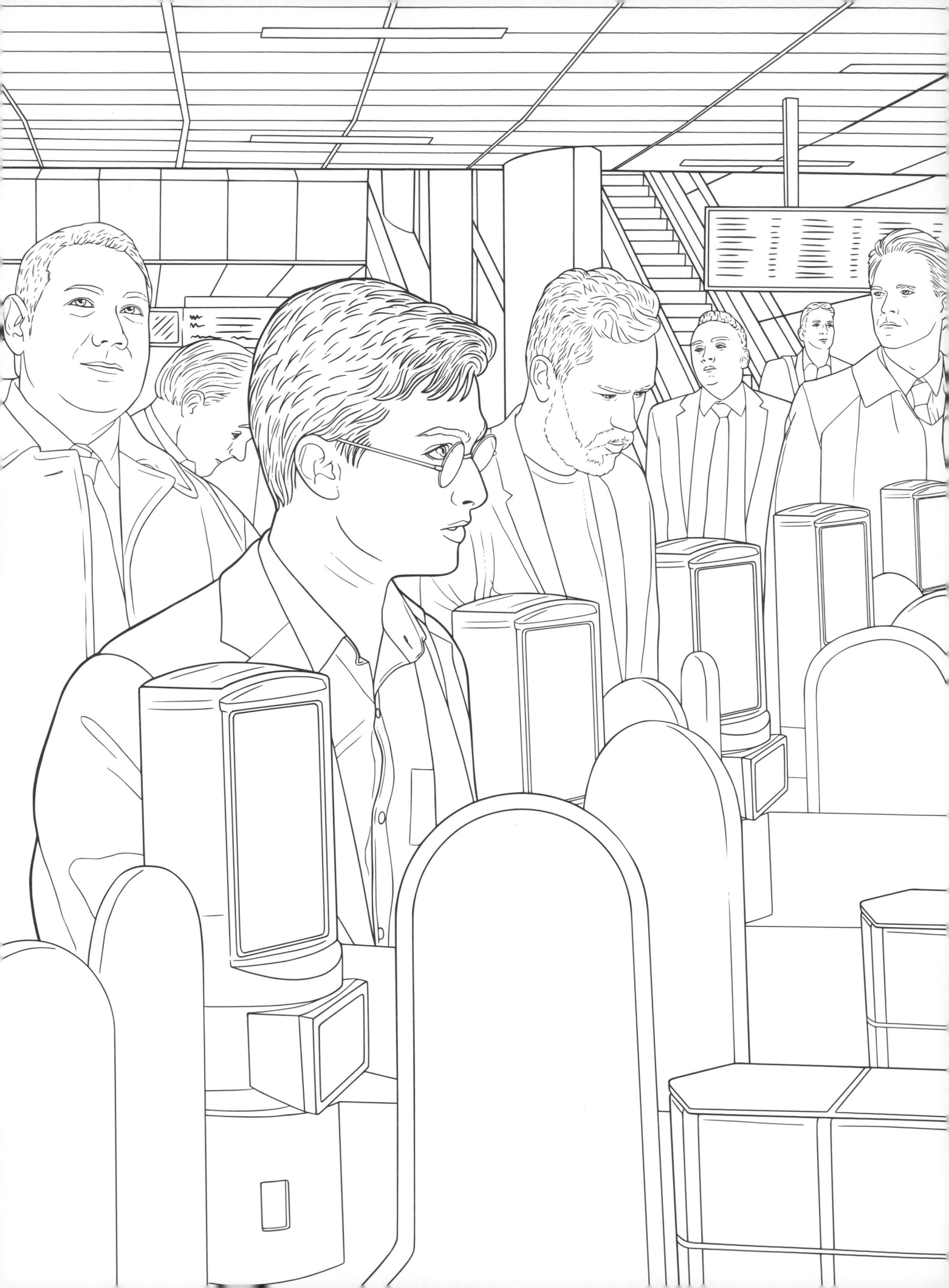

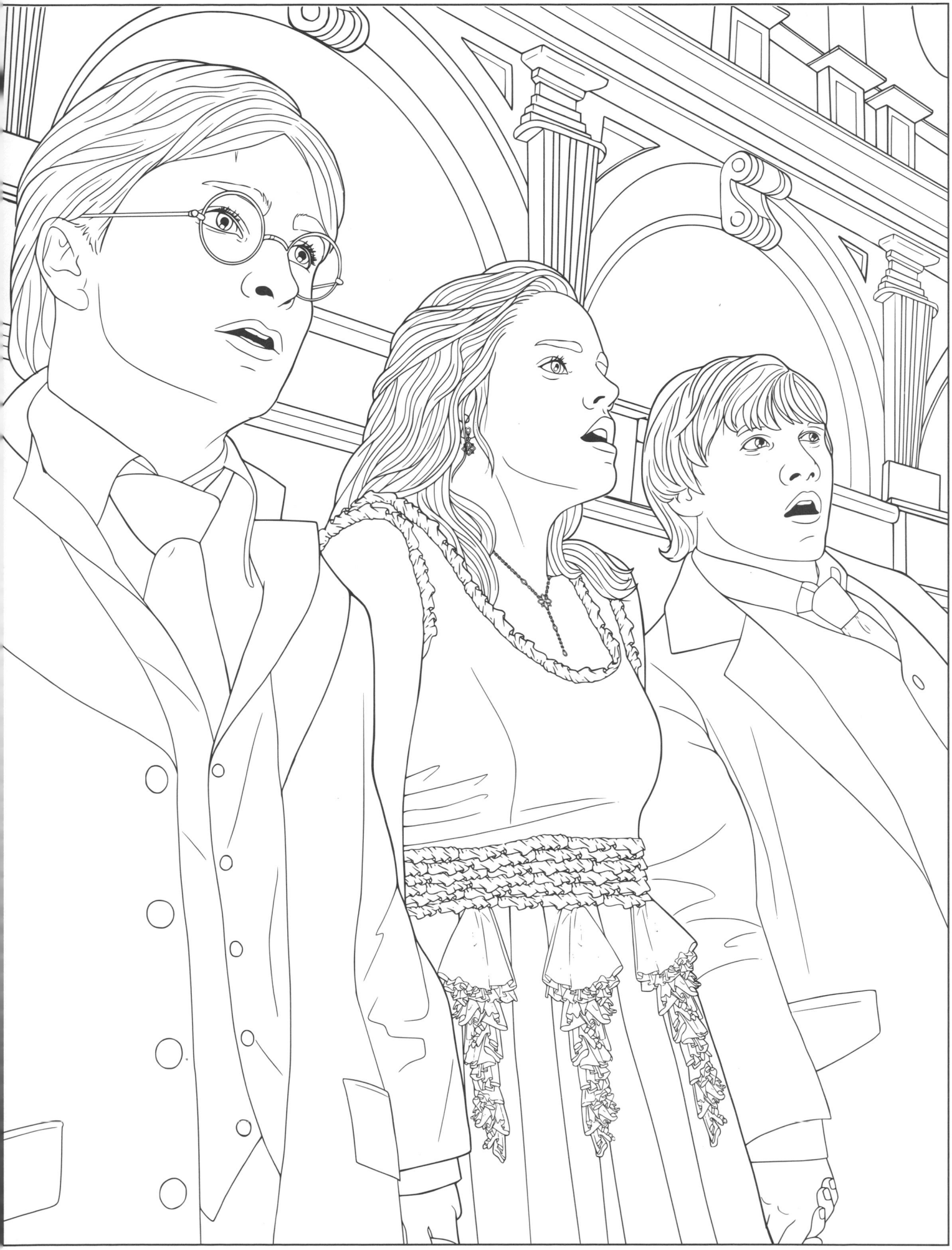

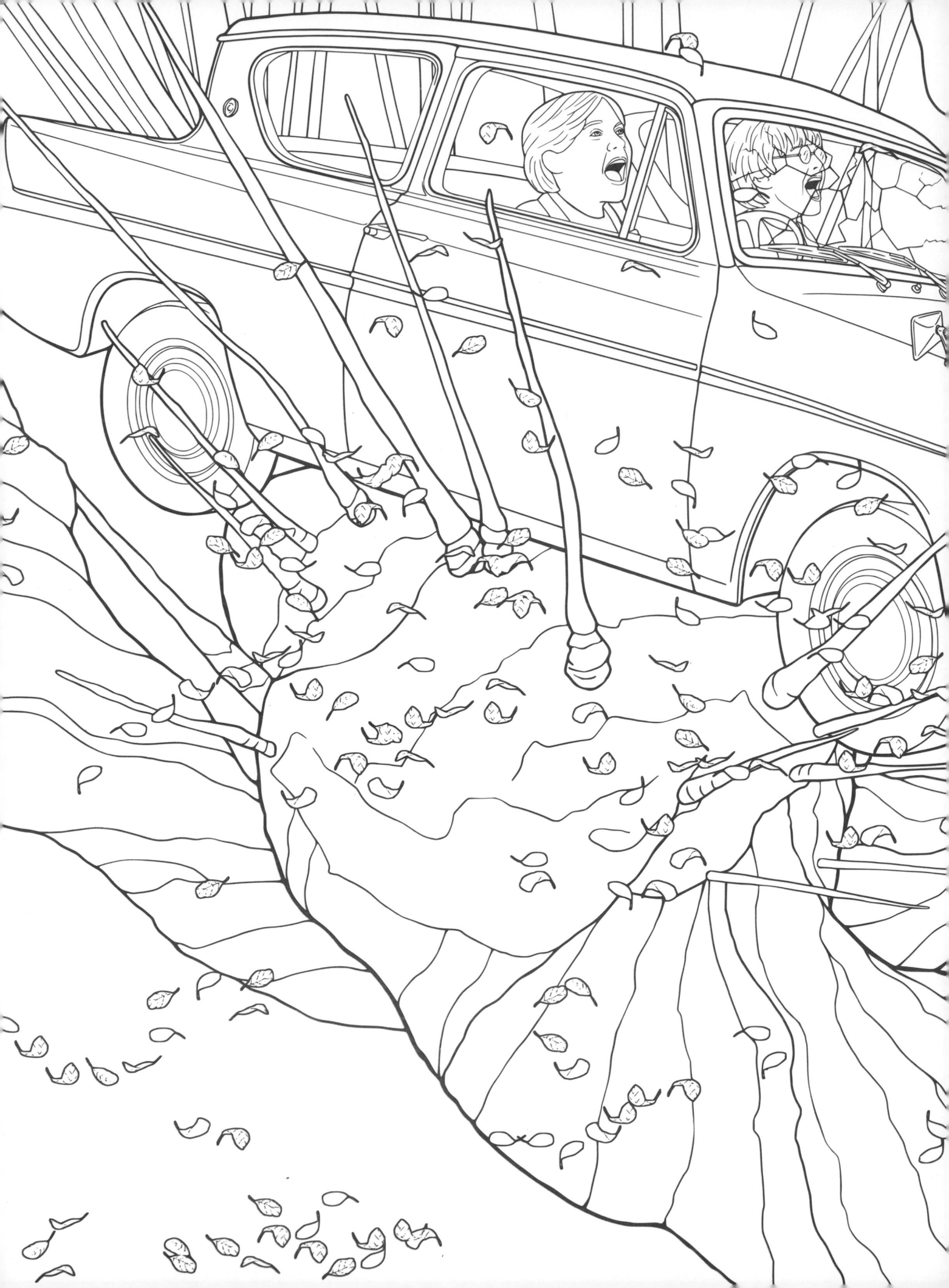

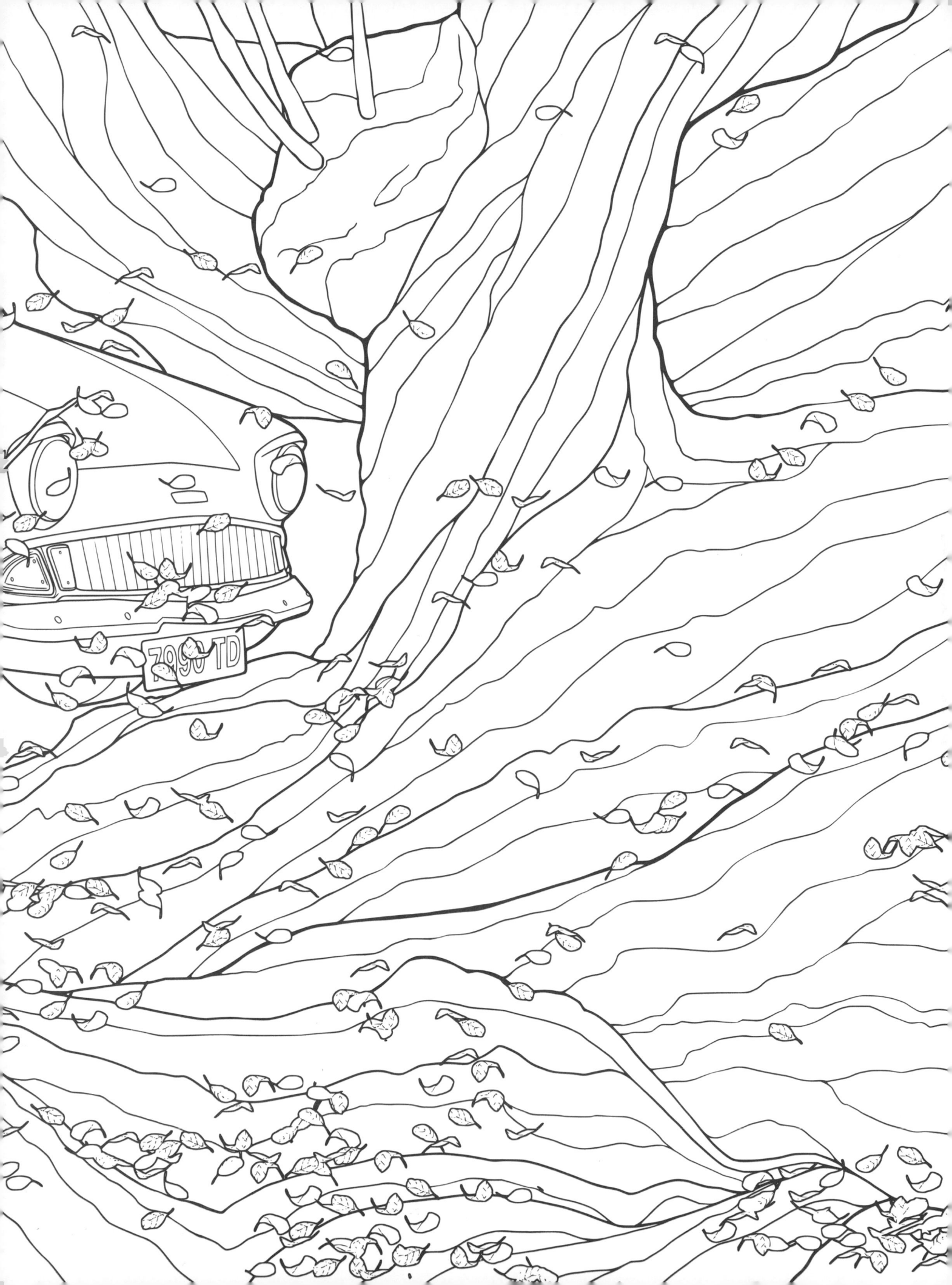
Z990 TD

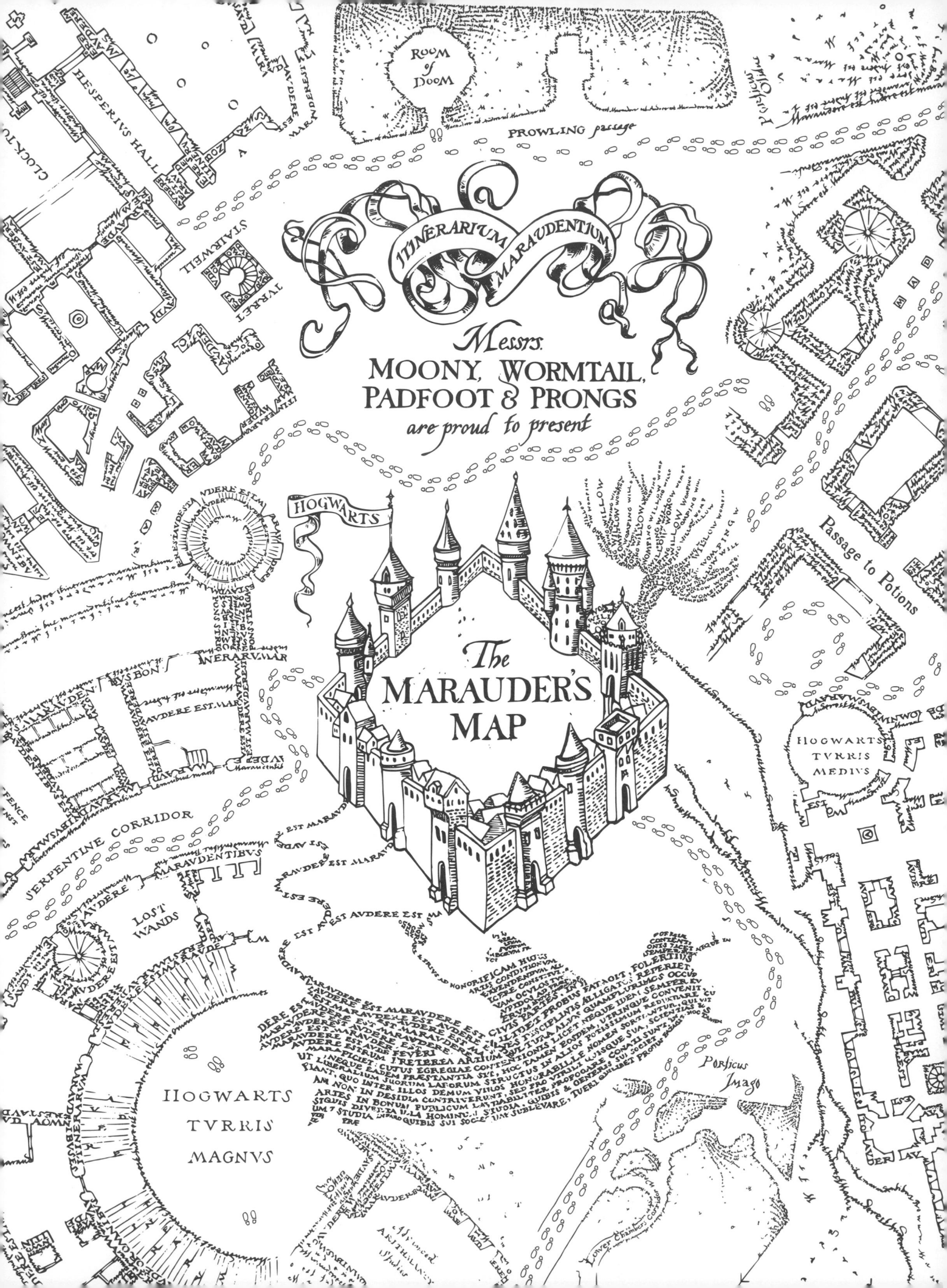
ITINERARIUM MARAUDENTIUM
Messrs.
MOONY, WORMTAIL, PADFOOT & PRONGS
are proud to present
The MARAUDER'S MAP
HOGWARTS
ROOM of DOOM
PROWLING passage
HESPERIUS HALL
CLOCK TOWER
STAIRWELL
Passage to Potions
HOGWARTS TURRIS MEDIUS
SERPENTINE CORRIDOR
LOST WANDS
HOGWARTS TURRIS MAGNUS
Porticus Imago

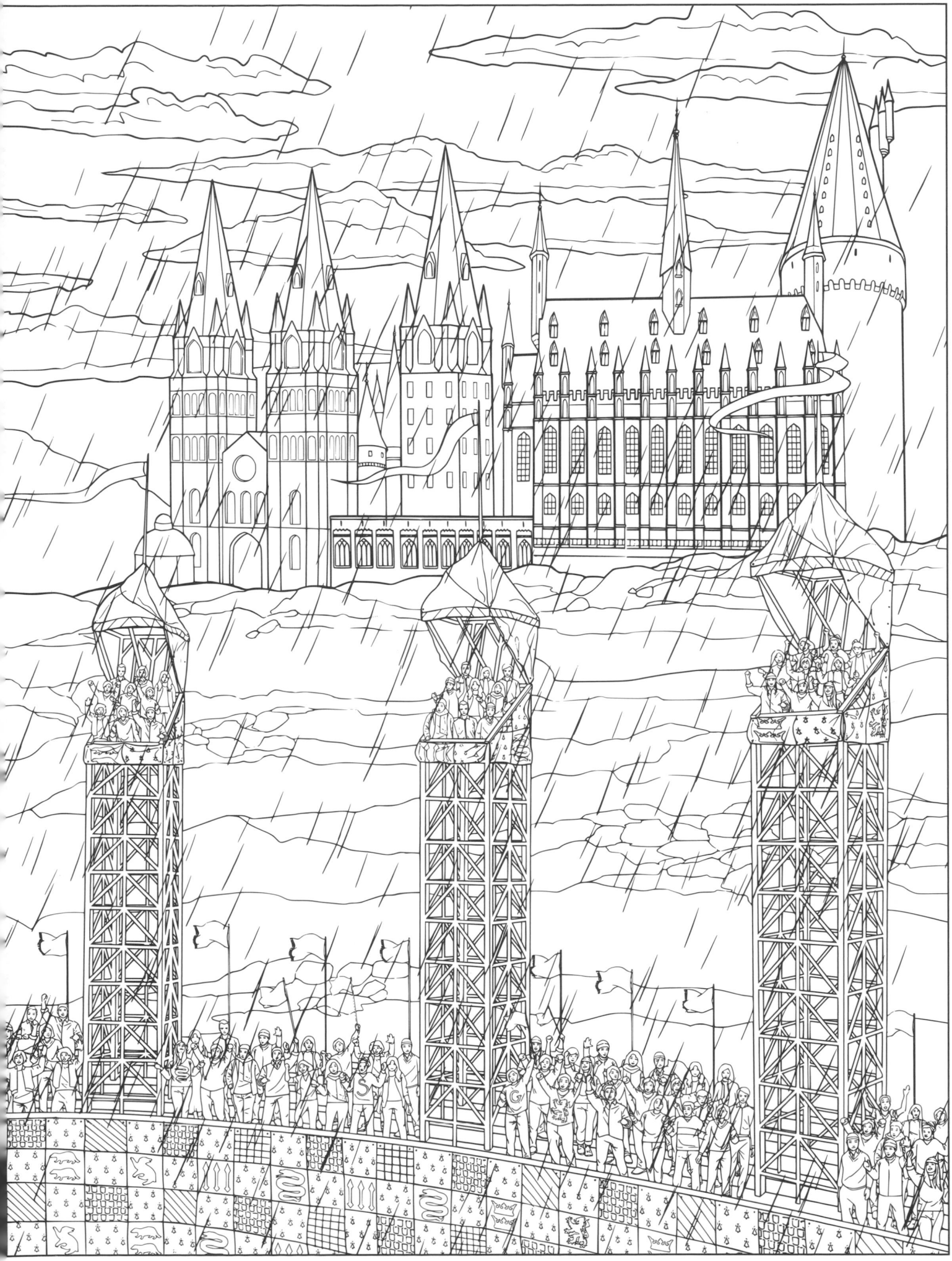

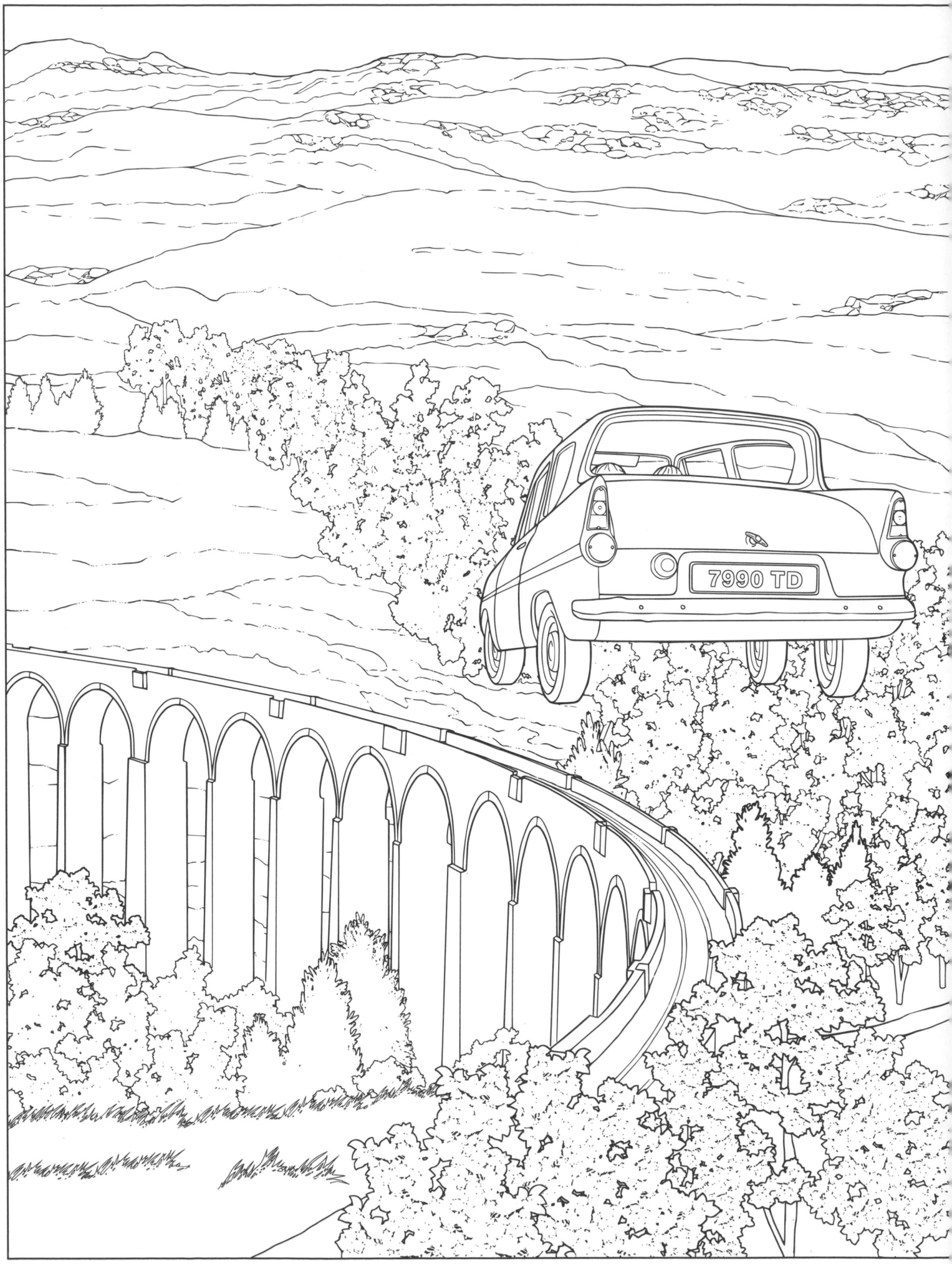
7990 TD

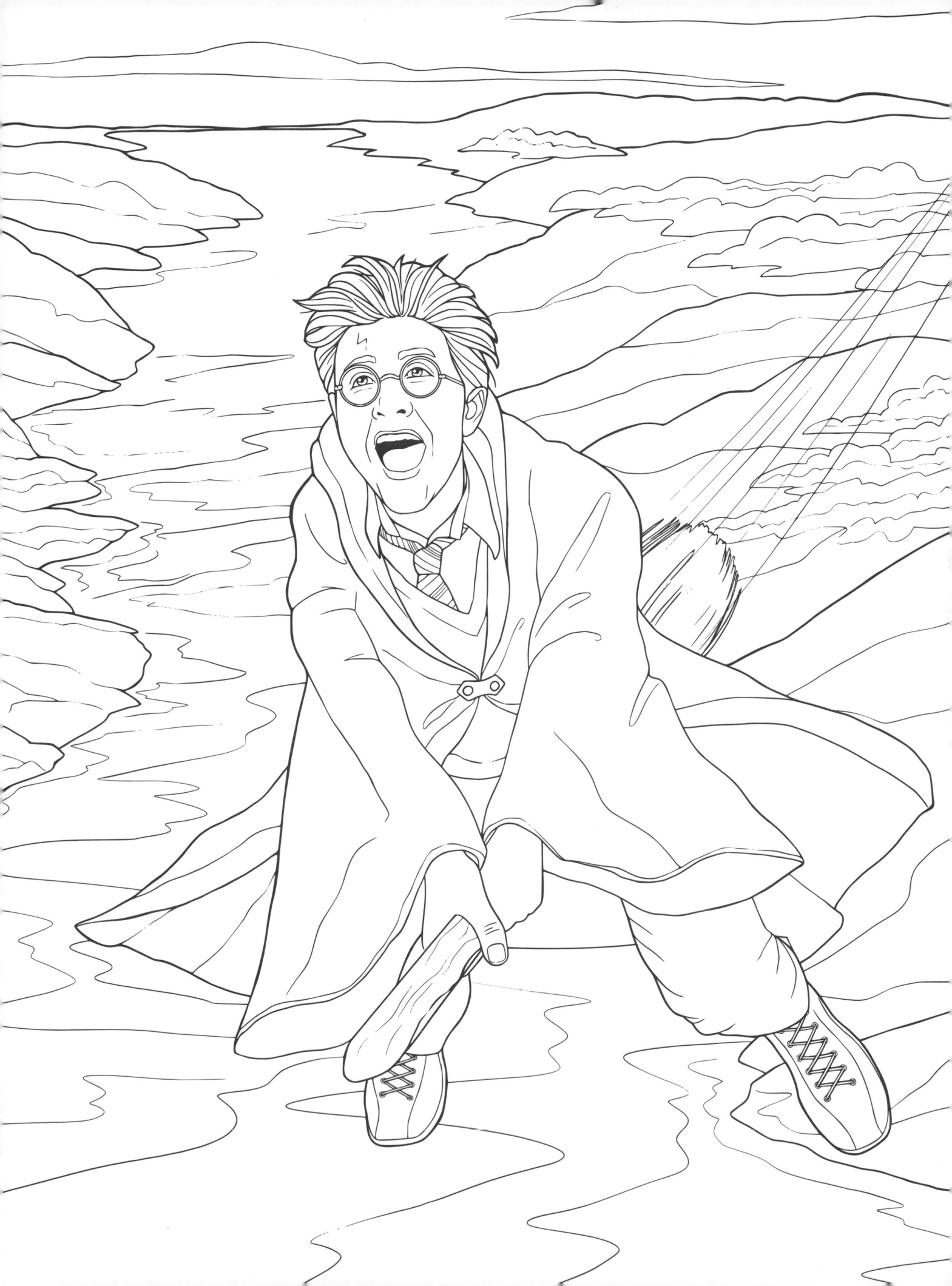

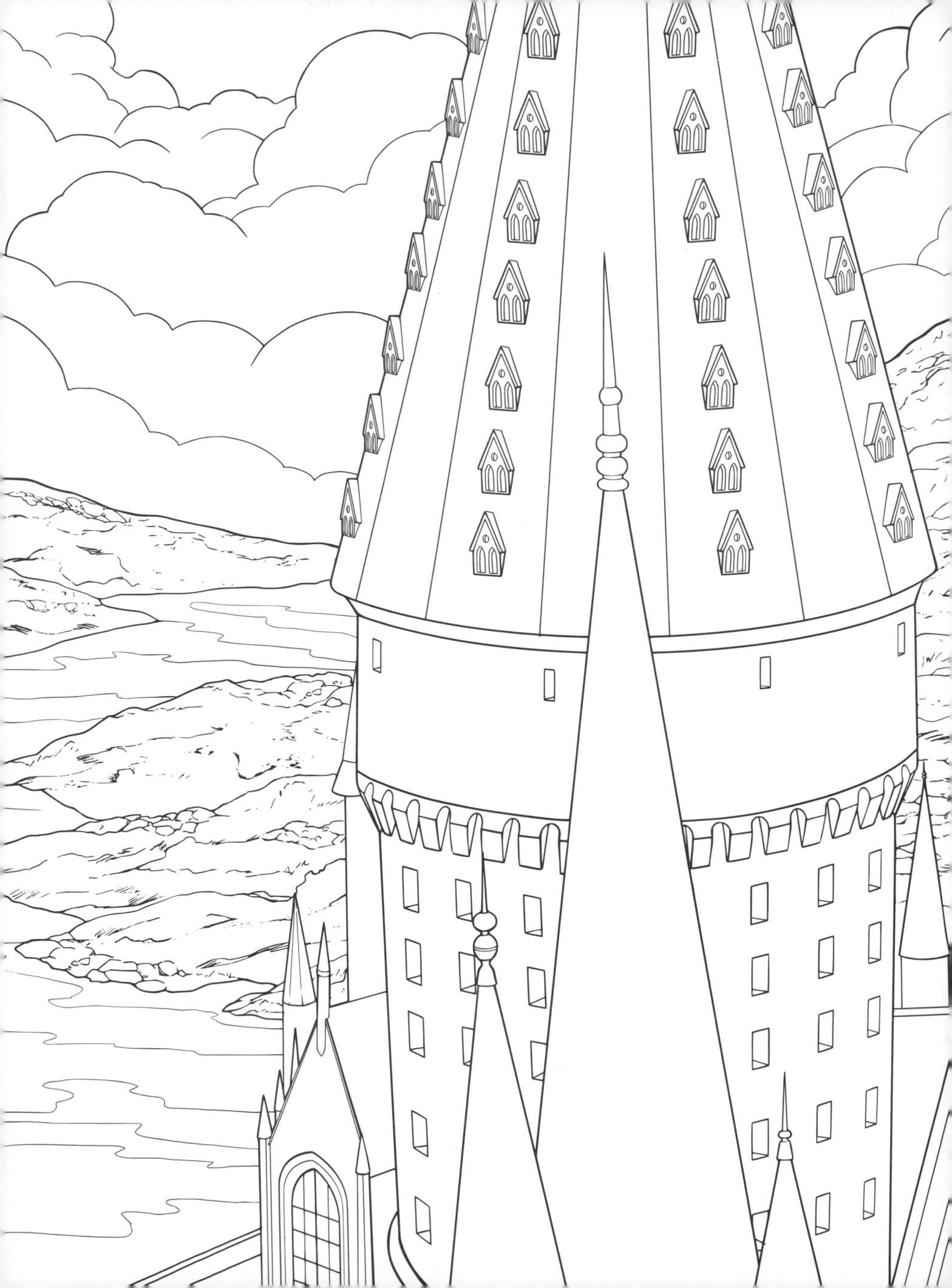

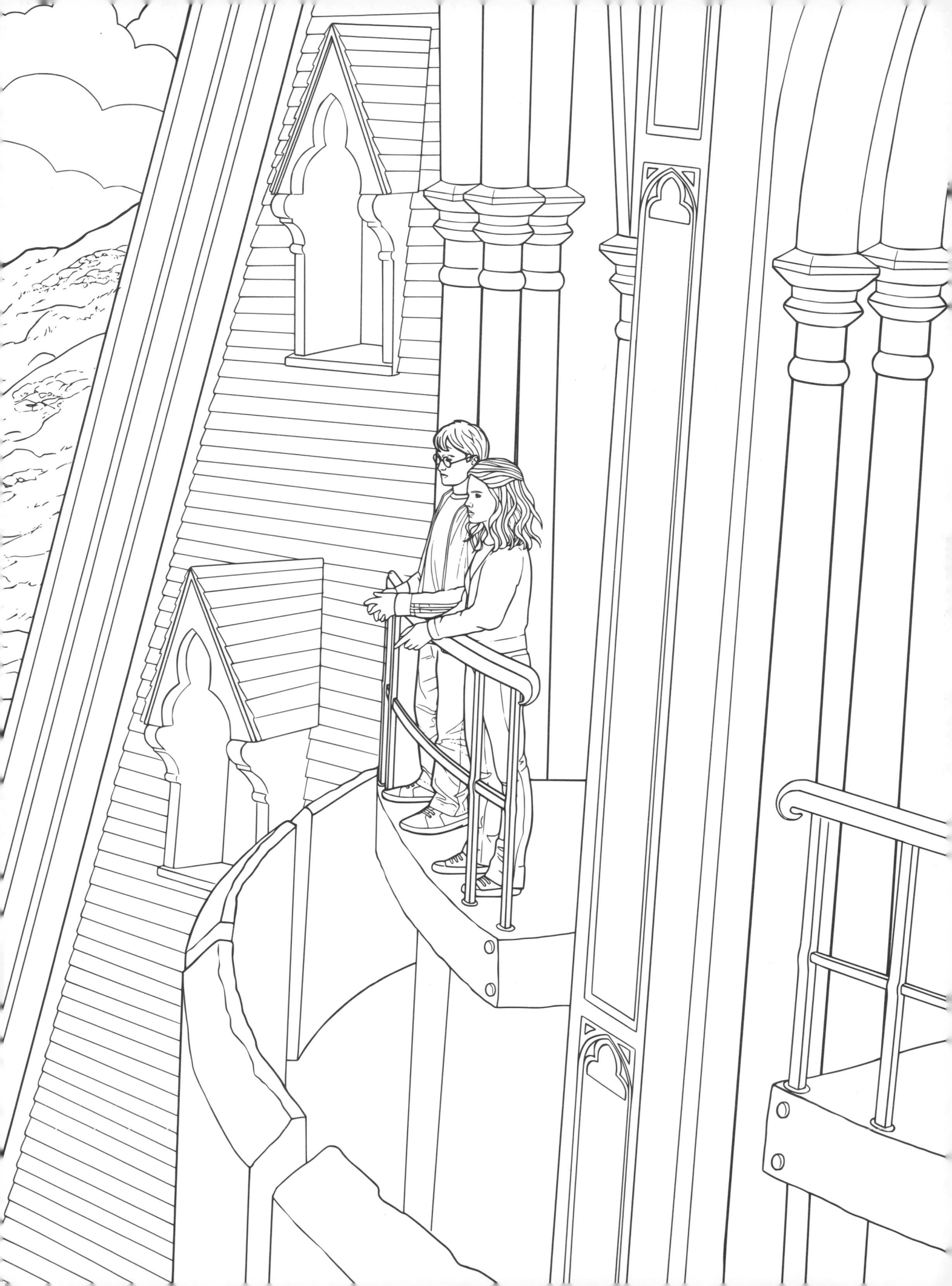

INSIGHT
EDITIONS

PO Box 3088
San Rafael, CA 94912
www.insighteditions.com

Find us on Facebook: www.facebook.com/InsightEditions
Follow us on Twitter: @insighteditions
Follow us on Instagram: @insighteditions

Copyright © 2023 Warner Bros. Entertainment Inc. WIZARDING WORLD characters, names and related indicia are © & ™ Warner Bros. Entertainment Inc. WB SHIELD: ™ & © WBEI. Publishing Rights © JKR. (s23)

All rights reserved. Published by Insight Editions, San Rafael, California, in 2023.

No part of this book may be reproduced in any form without written permission from the publisher.

ISBN: 979-8-88663-089-3

Publisher: Raoul Goff
VP, Co-Publisher: Vanessa Lopez
VP, Creative: Chrissy Kwasnik
VP, Manufacturing: Alix Nicholaeff
VP, Group Managing Editor: Vicki Jaeger
Publishing Director: Jamie Thompson
Senior Designer: Judy Wiatrek Trum
Editor: Stephen Fall
Editorial Assistant: Sami Alvarado
Senior Production Editor: Michael Hylton
Production Associate: Tiffani Patterson
Senior Production Manager, Subsidiary Rights: Lina s Palma-Temena

Page 11 Illustration of Harry and Hagrid on a flying motorcycle by Adam Raiti
All other Illustrations by Paula Rozelle Hanback

ROOTS of PEACE REPLANTED PAPER

Insight Editions, in association with Roots of Peace, will plant two trees for each tree used in the manufacturing of this book. Roots of Peace is an internationally renowned humanitarian organization dedicated to eradicating land mines worldwide and converting war-torn lands into productive farms and wildlife habitats. Roots of Peace will plant two million fruit and nut trees in Afghanistan and provide farmers there with the skills and support necessary for sustainable land use.

Manufactured in China by Insight Editions

10 9 8 7 6 5 4 3 2 1